THE STORI OF

Beaded Embellishment

Mary Stori

Martingale
& COMPANY

BOTHELL, WASHINGTON

CREDITS

President • Nancy J. Martin
CEO • Daniel J. Martin
Publisher • Jane Hamada
Editorial Director • Mary V. Green
Editorial Project Manger • Tina Cook
Technical Editor • Darra Williamson
Copy Editor • Karen Koll
Design and Production Manager • Stan Green
Illustrator • Laurel Strand
Cover and Text Designer • Trina Stahl
Photographer • Brent Kane

The Stori of Beaded Embellishment
© 2001 by Mary Stori

Martingale & Company
PO Box 118
Bothell, WA 98041-0118
www.martingale-pub.com

Printed in China
06 05 04 03 02 01   8 7 6 5 4 3 2 1

Library of Congress Cataloging-in-Publication Data

Stori, Mary
    The stori of beaded embellishment / by Mary Stori.
        p.   cm.
    ISBN 1–56477–339–6
    1. Fancy work. 2. Beadwork.   3. Embroidery.
4. Sewing.   I. Title.

TT750.S853 2001
746—dc21
                                                    00–05122

MISSION STATEMENT

*We are dedicated to providing quality products and service
by working together to inspire creativity
and to enrich the lives we touch.*

DEDICATION

❀

To the memory of Doreen Speckmann (1950–1999).
Her wit and humor sparkled like a thousand crystals!

ACKNOWLEDGMENTS

❀

As always, thank you to my two guys, husband David and son Chris,
for your love and support.

Editors are so vital to an author, and I'm indebted to Darra Williamson for her expertise.

I'm grateful to Terry Martin and all the other folks at Martingale & Company
for their dedication to quilters everywhere.

Thank you to Penny Taylor-Wallace of TWE/BEADS
for sharing her extensive knowledge of beads.

My appreciation is also extended to Pfaff American Sales Corporation,
Hobbs Bonded Fibers, and Primrose Gradations for their generosity.

Contents

PREFACE

THE EXISTENCE OF beads can be documented back to ancient times. Beads have played important roles in many religions. In fact, our English word *bead* may stem from Old English or Middle English words meaning *prayer*. Even today, both Hindus and Buddhists use a string of prayer beads and Catholics use a rosary to count prayers.

In addition to their use for spiritual meditation, beads have a rich history as a means of currency, mathematical calculation, and decoration for the body, clothing, and household furnishings. Beads can symbolize special events or recall a specific period of time, as with Mardi Gras beads, "love beads," and "worry beads."

This book isn't intended to be a history lesson about beads. As your interest grows, you may wish to investigate the vast quantity of related books available at your local library, bookstore, or in cyberspace. I wrote *The Stori of Beaded Embellishment* to share the techniques I've explored and developed as I've fallen in love with this fun medium. Be prepared to add a new dimension to your sewing skills as you too fall in love with beading on fabric!

INTRODUCTION

I HAVE TO confess: my interest in beadwork came as a total surprise to me! My style runs toward folk art, blue jeans, and antique country furniture. The glitz of sequins and the sparkle of beads brought Las Vegas or country-and-western entertainers to mind. I saw pearls and crystals only as lovely additions to wedding or prom dresses. My erroneous notion—that beadwork was confined to these specific categories—disappeared once I began using beads!

Beads can enhance your work by providing the "spark" that guides the eye around a piece. They can play the starring role in a design, as in a beaded spiderweb on a jacket, or fill a supporting role by enhancing a quilt's winter scene as beaded snowflakes. With only a few basic stitching methods, you can display countless embellishments on both quilts and garments.

You do not need any beading experience or special equipment. Beginners will feel confident as they follow the illustrated directions, while experienced stitchers are sure to be inspired by the many novel approaches offered. You'll learn to eliminate sagging beads, untidy thread ends, and puckered fabric!

GETTING STARTED

THE INFORMATION PRESENTED in this book prepares you to explore beading fabric surfaces. As eager as you may be to pick up a needle right now, please take the time to read the following chapters carefully first. Beads and embellishments may be completely new to many of you, so it makes sense to get acquainted with your materials before you begin a project.

ABOUT BEADS

WITHOUT GETTING too technical: if it has one hole, it can be categorized as a bead. My attitude has always been that *anything* with a hole in it is fair game to be incorporated into my work. For that matter, if it doesn't have a hole, I'm challenged (and happy) to make one.

Beads are available commercially at bead shops, craft and fabric stores, from conference and show vendors, and through mail-order sources. In addition, I never overlook "found" bead sources such as garage sales, flea markets, and antique stores.

One doesn't need to find "loose" beads either. Consider taking jewelry apart for its beads, as well as for other possible embellishments. Clothing, purses, wall hangings, and other finished products provide an additional source for unique beads.

Bead Materials

Using a variety of different types of beads adds interest to a finished piece, and these beads can be made from a dizzying array of materials. This makes it great fun to seek out beads to depict specific subjects for theme quilts.

Here are some of the most typical materials you are likely to encounter:

- *Glass* is the most common material used in manufacturing beads.

- Natural materials such as *bone, horn, wood, amber, ivory, coral,* and *pearls* are cut, polished, carved, and drilled into a variety of shapes and sizes. *Natural crystal quartz* beads can be purchased still in their "rough" state or already shaped.

- *Precious* and *semi-precious stones* are treasured for their basic beauty. While diamonds and emeralds can be budget busters, alternatives such as turquoise or jade chips make affordable substitutes.

- *Plastic* is often used to make fake "gems."

- In recent years, a version of polyvinyl chloride known as polymer clay has become popular as a means of creating a less expensive form of *ceramic* beads.

- *Gold, silver,* and *copper* have been used to make beads for centuries. Silver is widely used, but requires a coating (or maintenance afterwards) to avoid tarnishing. Copper is often stamped or die-cast into shapes, as are *brass* and *aluminum.*

Types and Sizes of Beads

Bead sellers are not always consistent when referring to different types of beads by name or finish. Fortunately, the materials required for most of my techniques and projects are fairly generic, so you can leave the worry about precision sizes and shapes to bead artists who make jewelry or other ornaments where the gauge is important. For instance, "air bubbles" for fish can be created with commonly available materials such as tiny seed beads, three-cuts, or even big pearls. My final selection is usually determined by the beads I have on hand.

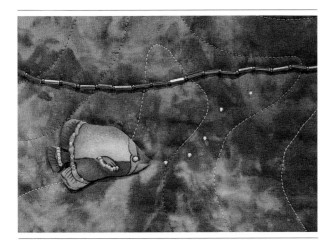

ISLAND HOPPING # 2 *(detail) by Mary Stori.*
Tiny seed beads depict air bubbles.

As with bead terminology, bead sizing may not be standard from one manufacturer to another. In other words, when you physically compare a specific bead by the size indicated on its packaging to a bead sizing chart that displays the "actual" bead size, the two may not match. Furthermore, sizes can sometimes vary within a single tube or package! Not to worry: for the methods and projects described in this book, small variances in size will generally not be noticeable, nor will they cause technical problems. If you should find it necessary, you can always re-sort or grade the beads as you work.

The following general terminology will be used to identify various types of beads throughout this book:

Seed beads were perhaps named for their literal resemblance to plant seeds. They are often known as *rocailles*, a French word meaning "little rocks," although some bead sellers still recognize the physical differences by name. (A seed bead is almost completely round, with a round hole, while the rocaille is a seed bead with a square hole.) You may even notice these beads labeled simply "small glass beads."

Seed bead size is identified by number, with the bead size decreasing as the size numbers grow larger. For example, a size #10 bead will be larger than a size #12 bead.

Most seed beads sold at bead shops in this country are size #11 and are sold by the hank.

Japanese cylinder beads are often mistaken for common seed beads. Though more costly, their advantages are many: they are consistent in size and perfectly cylindrical, with polished ends, thin walls, and a large hole for easy threading. The most common size is equivalent to our size #12 seed bead. You'll find these beads resold under trademark names such as "Antique," "Delicious," "Magnifica," and "Delicas."

Charlottes are also known as *true-cuts* or *one-cuts*. These Czech-made seed beads can be distinguished by the one or two small flat facets on their surface. *Three-cuts*, also made in the Czech Republic, feature irregular facets on their surface, although not necessarily three as the name implies. The name refers to the typical three-cut production process, during which the manufacturer guides raw-chopped pieces of glass cane through a grinding machine three times.

Bugle beads are segments of glass tube with a small diameter that is fairly consistent with a size #11 or #12 seed bead. They often have a smooth exterior, but can be found with outside ridges as well. One specific variety, called twisted bugles, appear ropelike, but are in fact smooth both inside and out. They're made by applying a unique spiral lining inside the bead, which increases the sparkle.

Bugles are sized by length, with the bead size increasing as the size numbers grow larger—the opposite of the sizing method used for seed beads. For example, a size #5 bugle bead will be larger than a size #2. Bugles may also be sized by millimeters, with a 30 mm bugle measuring about 1³⁄₁₆" long.

Broken or chipped beads are common with bugles, so I allow for extras in the project instructions.

Triangles are larger glass beads (usually size #5 but also available in sizes #8 and #10) with three rather rounded edges, hence their name. They are manufactured in Japan.

Bead Styles and Finishes

The following terms describe some of the more commonly used bead styles and finishes.

- An *opaque* bead is a solid-color bead. You cannot see through it.

- On the other hand, you can see through a *transparent* bead. Light passes completely through it, even when the bead is colored.

- *Color-lined* is easy to remember. These beads are either clear or colored glass on the outside with a contrasting colored lining.

- A *silver-lined* bead has its interior coated with a silver lining to reflect light through the transparent glass.

- *Iris* beads have a metallic look, like light reflecting off an oil slick.

- *Iridescent* beads have a multicolored, shiny finish.

- *Luster* beads are transparent, with a rich, shimmery finish.

- *Matte* refers to a dull or frosted finish.

- *Metallic* refers to a bead with a metallic coating, and should not be confused with beads made entirely from metal.

Tips for Buying Beads

Purchase the best-quality beads you can find. While price is naturally a factor, keep in mind that a less-expensive package may not be a savings at all if you have to discard many defective beads.

Look for beads that are uniform both in the outer measurement and in the size of the hole. Make note of the manufacturer's name to keep track of favorites, as well as to avoid future purchases of beads that disappoint you.

You'll find beads for sale by the strand or hank, loose by bulk weight, in tubes, and in small containers or packages. Some unique or specialty beads can be purchased individually.

A strand of identical beads can measure anywhere from 16" to 20" long. A hank is a grouping

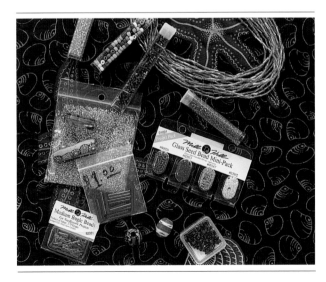

Beads and embellishment materials are packaged and sold in many ways.

of strands—usually twelve, but sometimes ten. Because I prefer to have a large variety of beads on hand, I'm partial to buying beads as "mixtures" or "collections," such as those sold by TWE/BEADS (see "Resources" on page 94). These are combinations of bead sizes, shapes, finishes, and colors organized and repackaged into tubes or other packaging by the seller. They are a good value when all you need is several dozen red beads—and not five hundred!

Craft and fabric stores should not be your only resource for beads. Check the yellow pages in your phone book for local bead shops where you can expect to see a large assortment of beads and obtain good advice. Review the list of resources provided in this book for both mail-order and online sources. These bead sellers have excellent catalogs and Web sites, complete with guidelines regarding bead sizes and styles.

Storing Beads

Use common sense regarding the storage of your bead collection. Whenever possible, store beads away from the light, in a cool, dry location. Avoid extreme conditions such as heat, humidity, and dampness. Some of my funky plastic beads became misshapen when I placed them too close to a heat source. It's a mistake I'm not likely to make again!

Most bead suppliers sell special bead organizers that work well for small collections. While convenient, the organizers can sometimes be costly. Here are some alternative, relatively inexpensive ideas to help you organize your stash of beads, as well as other embellishment items—such as charms, buttons, and doodads—that can be a challenge to store:

- Check hardware stores for storage units that are normally used for nuts and bolts. They come in a variety of sizes, and most have clear plastic drawers that slide out for easy access.

- In addition to hardware stores, look for compartmentalized plastic boxes in other out-of-the-way places, such as sporting-goods (fishing-tackle boxes) and toy departments (Matchbox car cases).

- Plastic storage cases designed for embroidery floss make good storage options. Select one with permanent rather than moveable dividers, which might allow beads to slip underneath, into an adjacent section.

- Recycle the sturdy clear plastic tubes or boxes in which beads are sold.

- Zipper-locking snack or sandwich bags work well for storing larger quantities of beads.

- Clean and reuse spice and herb bottles or jars for bulkier items such as buttons or charms.

- Empty film canisters are handy, too. When using an opaque canister, hot glue one bead to the lid to help you readily identify the contents.

PREPARING TO BEAD
Testing Materials

Many conditions can impact the long-lasting beauty of your beaded embellishments. For example, you may assume that beautiful pink twisted bugle bead has been made from pink glass and the color will remain true forever. However, it's possible that the interior has been dyed, which means that the color can fade with light, disappear with water and detergent, or become stripped due to dry cleaning. This isn't to say all pink beads will be a problem, but it's one of the colors I'm especially cautious about.

Sequins are very likely to lose their color if washed or dry cleaned. Silver-lined beads are desired for their lovely sparkle, but be wary, for as the lining tarnishes, the bead may darken and dull. Some beads with metallic finishes not only react poorly to washing, but may also change color due to a chemical reaction to your hands. They may react adversely to heat, or the finish may rub or flake off due to friction.

So what can you do to avoid disappointments? You've already taken a big step by reading this section and becoming aware that not all bead colors and finishes are stable or permanent. The second—and most important—step is to test. *I cannot stress this enough: Test beads before beginning a project!*

Check for colorfastness by soaking a few beads in a small bowl of *hot* water and dishwashing liquid for a few hours, and then comparing them to the originals. Some bead experts recommend putting cheesecloth in the bottom of the bowl so it can be checked for dye residue as well. If you are using beads on a project that may be dry cleaned someday, stitch a few to an item that will be cleaned, then examine the result. Better to test before you spend time sewing on a zillion pearls, only to find that the dry-cleaning chemicals have removed the pearl coating!

Another good test is to place a small number of beads on a sunny windowsill for about two weeks. Checking them against the original color should give you a good indication as to whether they are lightfast.

Unlike beads used in jewelry that rests upon the body, beads used on quilts or garments should not be harmed by chemical reactions to perfume or lotions. However, the heat or steam from an iron can strip away color and finishes, so always be cautious during the construction of any project and when touching up with an iron afterwards.

Basic Supplies

One of the greatest advantages to beadwork is its portability. The supplies and equipment requirements are fairly minimal. In fact, you may already have many of the necessary items in your sew-ing room. For additional information, see "Resources" on page 94.

Beads, charms, buttons, crystals, sequins, and so forth: These are a must. Start collecting today!

Needles: This is going to surprise you: I don't use standard long beading needles, because I find they are difficult to manipulate and bend too easily. Instead, I prefer to use a size #11 or #12 quilting Between. This short, strong needle is perfect when beading one stitch at a time. The second type of needle I use is an appliqué, Sharp, or Straw needle, again usually a size #11 or #12. This longer, very thin needle works well when a beading technique calls for passing through the bead more than once, or when using beads with very tiny holes.

Nymo Beading Thread: This waxed nylon thread is a super-strong, yet fairly fine thread. Although it is available in several sizes, I use size "D" exclusively because I like its weight. It comes in many colors as well. I usually use white, black, or gray thread, matching the thread to the bead color and/or value, with gray being medium. To reduce excess twisting of Nymo thread, prestretch it by gently pulling it inch by inch after the needle is threaded.

Embroidery scissors or small sharp thread snips: These allow you to cut sharply angled thread ends, which makes it easier to thread the eye of the needle. Additionally, you'll have more control when trimming thread tails close to the fabric.

Hoop or PVC frame: To maintain fabric and thread tension, and ensure a pucker- and distortion-free project, place your work in an embroidery hoop, a hand-held quilting hoop, or a PVC-type lap frame whenever possible.

✍

When stitching a large number of beads to a project, it may not be possible to secure the top hoop or the PVC clips without damaging the existing embellishments. Try my nifty trick: position the fabric as usual over the bottom hoop or frame. Instead of using the top hoop or the PVC clips, wrap the excess fabric over (and slightly under) the edges of the hoop or frame to meet on the reverse side. Secure these layers together from the top with safety pins, as close to the edge of the hoop or frame as possible. This creates adequate tension, even on large quilts. Reposition as necessary.

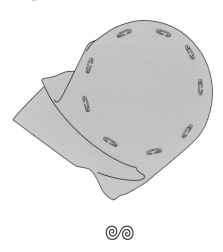

✍

Additional Helpful Information

Good lighting helps to avoid eyestrain. A nice, bright light, positioned to reduce shadows, allows you to bead for hours.

Find a comfortable place to work, whether at a table or in your favorite chair. I sit on our couch with my feet resting on the coffee table in front of me. Resting my hoop on a lap board also helps to keep my shoulders from getting tense and sore.

You'll want containers to hold the beads as you stitch. Here are some nifty options to keep things going smoothly:

- The low sides and smooth surface of small shallow glass or ceramic dishes make it easy to dip in and pop the needle through the hole of the bead. Some hard plastic containers work well too. Avoid more flexible plastic containers because the tip of the needle will create nicks and gouges as you scoop up the beads. This eventually dulls the needle, and slows you down as the needle catches on these flaws.

- Place beads-in-waiting on a scrap of leather, rough side up, on your lap board. The beads are visible, ready to be threaded onto the needle, and the leather prevents them from rolling off the board.

- When working with a variety of beads at one time, use a miniature muffin tin to separate them while keeping each type handy.

- Spills can and do happen, and picking up tiny beads is annoying. Try one of my favorite tricks. Place a large, shallow jelly-roll pan on your lap or table as you work. If an accident happens, the beads will most likely fall into the pan and not on the carpet!

- Here's a suggestion that always gets knowing nods when I mention it in workshops: Have your eyesight examined! Because doctors test for reading distance, and *not* sewing distance, I recommend you bring your hoop along to demonstrate how and where you will be holding it. I have option A, B, and C glasses; it seems every task requires a different pair! Sometimes "cheater" magnifying glasses from the drugstore do the trick as well.

Finally, keep your mental health in mind! Some days my fingers are not attached to my brain, and frustration sets in quickly. The next day will be better, so instead I tackle one of the other zillions of tasks waiting for me . . . like scrubbing the toilets!

TECHNIQUES

PRELIMINARY CONSIDERATIONS

THIS CHAPTER FEATURES both written instructions and numerous illustrations to teach you the craft of attaching beads and other embellishments to fabric. For further inspiration and clarification, I've included photo examples of how these skills translate to my work. I think you will find the impact of incorporating beading techniques into your work so exciting, you won't want to stop!

As a self-taught embellishment enthusiast, I've adapted some traditional methods used by bead artists who create objects such as jewelry, vessels, or sculptures. However, instead of working free-form on a loom or an object, my beadwork is done directly on fabric surfaces.

You may have heard the term *bead embroidery*, which generally refers to the process of incorporating beads while sewing decorative embroidery stitches onto fabrics. Depending upon the source, there are variations to the definition of bead embroidery, as well as to how the various stitches are sewn. Some of the designs offered here are based on traditional embroidery stitches, but because I've often found my own path, most are not. The terminology may be familiar but the end results will probably surprise you.

Construction Guidelines

As a general rule, I embellish the completed quilt top before sandwiching it with backing. I bead garments before they are assembled. The advantage to this approach is that all the stitches—and there can be a ton!—will be hidden in the quilt sandwich or by the garment's lining.

Embellishments can get heavy and the weight may distort the fabric. When planning projects that feature concentrated beading or significantly sized ornaments, it's a good idea to use a stabilizer on the wrong side of the fabric. The construction method I plan for the project usually determines the choice of stabilizer. Appliqué quilts, for instance, lend themselves to a layer of muslin. On the other hand, one way to add sturdiness to a pieced quilt top is to baste batting to the wrong side, then treat the two layers as one when you embellish. The cool thing is, your batting is now already in place! When you are finished beading, just add the backing fabric and quilt.

A good stabilizing choice for clothing is fusible tricot interfacing, which will maintain the drape of the garment.

Questions about quilting undoubtedly have entered your mind by now, particularly the questions "how" and "when." Embellished quilts constructed and stabilized in the manner described above are most easily quilted by hand. Embellishments interfere with the presser foot when you are machine quilting, especially when free-motion stitching, and are apt to be ripped off in the process! If you want to try machine quilting, it's best to keep the decorations to a minimum and place them very carefully.

Another option is to make and quilt the quilt sandwich in the traditional fashion and add the embellishments last, penetrating all three layers with the attaching thread. Since embellished quilts are usually destined for the wall anyway, just ignore the mess on the back. If that is not an option for you, it *is* possible to catch only the top two layers with the needle as you stitch. This requires more patience, though once you get the knack of it, it's not terribly difficult. The bottom line is that often the individual project will dictate your approach. Remember: you are in charge of the needle and thread, so don't be afraid to use the method that suits your work style the best.

When your beaded design requires you to mark the fabric with a specific pattern, please be sure to test your marking tool. Washing is the most common method for removing marks, and not all beads and embellishments are washable, so you'll want to keep that in mind when choosing your marker. I like to mark with soap slivers because—except on very light fabrics—soap is easily visible, can be dabbed off with a damp cloth if necessary, and acts almost like silicone to help the needle glide through the fabric. Granted, it's a little more difficult to draw very precise, narrow lines, but most of my designs don't require a flawless line anyway! When you must have precise lines, try transferring the design to tissue paper, pinning it to the project, and beading through the paper. This delicate paper has a tendency to tear away prematurely when you are working on large or concentrated patterns, so handle it carefully. I've also had fairly good luck beading small designs through marked freezer paper pressed onto fabric. In any event, always test your marking equipment to prevent disappointments!

I prefer working with a single length of thread approximately 12" to 16" long. Yes, you must rethread more often, but if the thread breaks there will be less to repair! Longer thread tangles more easily, and frays as it is pulled through the fabric again and again and again.

A final important reminder: for the best results, work in a hoop or frame whenever feasible, keeping the fabric as taut as possible. In my workshops, students practice the stitches by creating a sampler on an inexpensive 8" or 10" wooden embroidery hoop fitted with muslin. Consider

following along as I describe each stitch, and bead your own "reference library."

Hand and Hoop Position

My lack of formal training in beadwork has permitted much guilt-free experimentation because I have never been locked into specific "dos" and "don'ts." I discovered I achieved more accuracy when stitching from top to bottom (vertically) than when working along a horizontal plane (the usual method). When sewing horizontally—from right to left for instance—your stitching hand can obscure your vision in terms of where to place the needle.

On the other hand, when using my method and working toward yourself, your stitching hand is below the bead, making it much easier to see. For this reason, I always work toward myself when I'm using the basic bead stitch to embellish, whether it's to sew a single bead, a straight line, a curve, or a scatter stitch.

Think of your hoop as the face of a clock, with the screw at twelve o'clock and the bottom of the frame directly below at six o'clock. This orientation will come in handy as I describe the methods I use for the various beading stitches.

Basic Stitches and How to Use Them

Lock Stitch

Always use the lock stitch when starting a new thread. Thread the needle and knot one thread end, leaving a ⅛" tail. Enter the fabric from the wrong side, passing the needle through to the right side where the first bead is to be placed. Count about three threads of the fabric weave below the point where the thread has emerged, and push the needle back through the fabric to the wrong side. Count about three threads of the weave below the point where the thread has passed to the wrong side of the fabric, and return the needle to the right side. This lock stitch helps to take the strain off the thread and prevents the knot from popping up through the fabric.

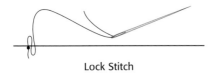

Lock Stitch

Basic Bead Stitch

The basic bead stitch is actually a back stitch, which secures each and every bead while automatically maintaining the thread tension.

Make a lock stitch as described above. Next, thread a bead onto the threaded needle, drawing the bead down to the surface of the fabric. Reinsert the needle into the fabric, taking a stitch that is one bead width toward the twelve o'clock side of the bead.

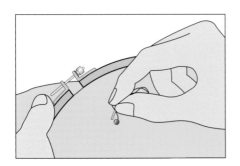

Draw the thread completely through to the wrong side so the bead covers the lock stitch. Come up from the wrong side of the fabric, taking a stitch that is one bead width from the six o'clock side of the bead you have just stitched. The hole will not be facing you, but will be parallel to the fabric so that it resembles a train tunnel.

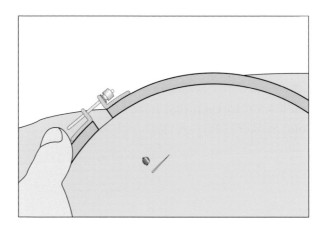

This basic stitch works on any type of bead. On a bugle bead, for example, the needle enters the right side of the fabric *one bugle-bead length* away, on the twelve o'clock side.

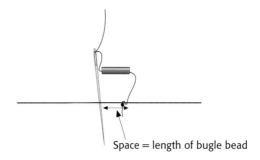

Space = length of bugle bead

Don't worry! After a little practice you'll be able to judge these distances easily.

Here's an easy way to remember my system for making basic beading stitches. After stringing a bead (or beads), always reinsert the needle into the background fabric on the twelve o'clock side of the bead. When reemerging to the right side of the fabric to add a new bead, always come up on the six o'clock side of the previous bead.

꩜

TYING OFF: THE PERFECT KNOT

If you are not already familiar with this knot, you are just going to love knowing about it! I use it as an all-purpose knot to end my thread for all hand sewing, with the exception of hand quilting. Here's how to do it for beading:

As you complete your last stitch, pull the needle and thread completely through to the wrong side of the fabric. While still on the wrong side, take a tiny stitch through the fabric, staying underneath the last bead so the stitch doesn't show.

Wrong side of fabric

Now pull the thread almost—but not completely—through, leaving a 2" loop.

Holding the needle by the eye, slide the tip and shank of the needle into the loop, entering from the fabric side. Rotate the needle over the thread, so that the thread wraps around the shank of the needle. Rotate the needle again to go back under the thread. Pull the needle through the spiral until a snug knot forms on the fabric. (The movement of the needle is under, over, and then under the thread.) Trim the thread tail to approximately ⅛".

BEADING A STRAIGHT LINE

Continue adding beads in the same manner as described for the basic bead stitch, and you will have mastered the next step: beading a straight line! You can mark a line to follow or eyeball it, as I often do. When the line of beads has reached the desired length, pass the needle through to the wrong side of the fabric and tie off with a knot. It's as easy as that.

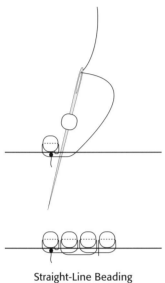

Straight-Line Beading

BEST FRIENDS *(detail) by Mary Stori.*
The letters "t" and "i" are examples of single straight-line beading. For a full view of the quilt, see page 59.

Crooked lines of beading result when the needle is not reinserted into the right side of the fabric directly in line with the previous bead. Be sure to reinsert the tip of the needle carefully. One thread of the fabric weave from the previous stitch is a good rule of thumb. Be careful not to pierce the thread of the previous stitch, however, since this can weaken or split the thread.

BEAD EMBROIDERY

One accepted procedure for what is described as bead embroidery consists of stringing several beads onto the thread at one time and backstitching through only the last bead of each series. I prefer the control and sturdiness of the basic bead stitch, although the other method is faster. I recommend that you use the bead-embroidery method only when excessive repetition of the basic bead stitch might cause puckering of a very lightweight fabric. Another exception might be to reduce sewing time when the entire fabric surface is to be covered with beads.

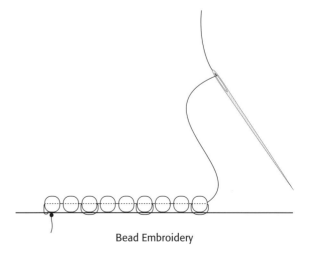

Bead Embroidery

BEADING A CURVED LINE

Use the basic bead stitch to bead lines that curve. Position the first bead as described in the instructions for the basic stitch (see page 15). After the first bead is in place, bring the needle up on the six o'clock side of the bead, one bead width away. Add the next bead, making sure to aim the needle downward so that it reenters the background fabric one thread of the fabric weave from the previous stitch. It is vital to aim for that previous thread to ensure that the bead will "sit" correctly in line along the curve. Just be sure that you do not pierce the thread!

When stitching curves, you may have a slightly altered perspective of one bead width at first, but soon the measurement will become familiar. Keep the following strategy in mind: Always make the correction to accommodate the curve when the needle comes up through the background fabric, not when it goes down. This isn't too difficult if you are following a marked curved line since you tend to follow the curve naturally, but it's helpful to understand the mechanics nonetheless.

BEADING QUICK CURVED LINES

Follow the directions for stitching a curved line as described at left, but after each seed bead, add one bugle bead as illustrated below. As in regular curved-line beading, this will require getting the knack of how to judge the space required by the bead on a curve—in this case, a bugle bead. I don't consider it cheating to simply lay a bugle bead in position to help judge where the needle should come up from the wrong side of the fabric.

Since a bugle bead can cover more space in one stitch than a typical seed bead, consider using this quick method when your overall design is large, when the curved line is long, or when you want to accomplish the beading more quickly.

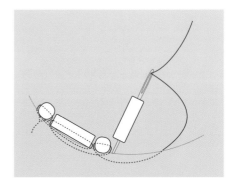

Quick Curved Beading

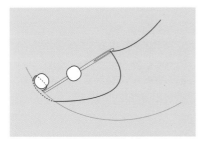

Curved-Line Beading

CAUGHT IN THE WEB *(detail) by Mary Stori.*
An example of quick curved beading. Alternate bugle beads and seed beads make the work go faster. For a full view of the quilt, see page 49.

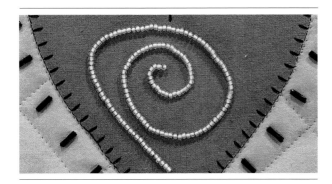

BEST FRIENDS *(detail) by Mary Stori. An example of curved-line beading. For a full view of the quilt, see page 59.*

It is easier to achieve neat, tight curves in quick curved beading if you think of seed beads as "spacer" beads. Rather than stitching just one (and then a bugle bead), try sewing several along a tight curve before adding the next bugle bead. You can then proceed with the usual quick curved beading method.

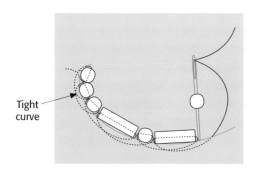

Tight curve

Straightening and Strengthening Lines of Beading

The following technique serves a dual purpose. It can be used to improve the appearance of either straight or curved beaded lines by straightening beads that may be slightly crooked. You'll also find it useful for building in extra strength, especially when beading garments, which are naturally subjected to more wear and tear than a wall quilt. You'll want to use a fine appliqué needle for this technique.

Stitch the complete line of beading as usual, tying off the thread on the wrong side. Bring a new thread up from the wrong side of the fabric, just underneath the last bead. (You'll probably want to avoid starting the new thread with a lock stitch, which can be difficult to hide under the line of beads.) Enter the "tunnel" of beads, running the threaded needle through the beads, and exiting a bead when it becomes difficult to travel farther; for example, when the distance you need to travel exceeds the length of the needle. Do not take a stitch into the fabric. Instead, pull the threaded needle completely through that bead, maneuver the needle as necessary, and go right back into the next bead in the line. Continue until you reach the end of the line. Give the thread a slight tug, and the beads will adjust themselves properly.

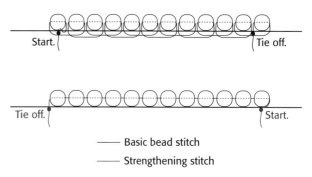

Start. / Tie off.

Tie off. / Start.

—— Basic bead stitch
—— Strengthening stitch

Whenever possible, it's best to straighten and strengthen lines with one long, continuous thread. Taking a tie-off stitch between the beads creates a tiny gap in the beaded line.

Scatter Stitch

Beads don't need to be the focus of the quilt. Sometimes just a little sparkle is all that's required. Broadcasting (or scattering) them over the fabric surface is an effective method for achieving that goal. To help with continuity, you can follow a line that has been drawn or sewn on the fabric.

Begin with the lock stitch, followed by one basic bead stitch. Now bring the needle up to the right side of the fabric, anywhere between ¼" to 1½" from the first bead. It isn't important that these subsequent distances are evenly spaced, or even that the same type of bead is used; just bead whatever looks appealing to you. Since the thread travels longer-than-usual distances beneath the fabric between beads, be sure to pull the thread completely through the fabric to ensure proper tension.

You can also scatter stitch in a zigzag pattern to create the appearance of random placement. Be sure to use the basic bead-stitch method of backstitching, adding each new bead below the previous one. It's easy! Just pay attention to the stitching order, and it's a snap to add twinkle to your pieces.

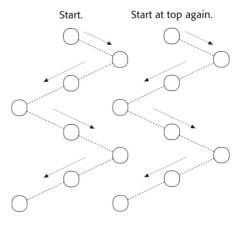

Scatter Stitch (Zigzag)

Scatter Stitch (Straight)

Waiting for Spring *(detail) by Mary Stori.*
An example of scatter-stitched lines. Random beading along the machine-quilted lines accentuates the sense of blowing wind. For a full view of the quilt, see page 47.

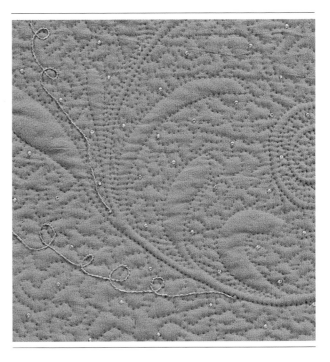

Spring Green *(detail) by Mary Stori.*
An example of scatter stitch in a zigzag pattern. The glimmer of small color-lined seed beads draws the eye around the quilt. For a full view of quilt, see page 44.

The Washer/Nut Method

The washer/nut method is so versatile, you'll use it again and again. Think of the embellishment you wish to add as the "washer," and the bead—which must be larger than the hole of the "washer"—as the "nut." To continue the hardware analogy, the thread acts as the "bolt."

LARGE BEADS

Now let's examine how the washer/nut method works for attaching beads. Begin with the lock stitch, and then string one large bead onto the thread. Follow the large bead with a smaller bead, remembering that the smaller bead must be larger than the hole of the first, large bead.

Pass the needle back through the hole of the large bead, bypassing the small bead. Pull the thread completely through to the wrong side of the fabric and tie off with a knot.

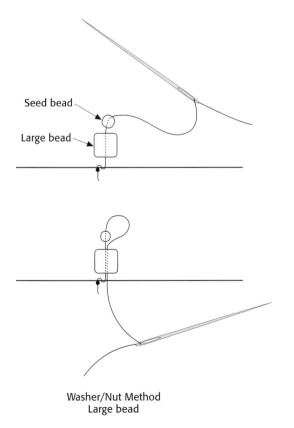

Seed bead
Large bead

Washer/Nut Method
Large bead

SEQUINS

These sparkly gems can be effective, but their impact is reduced when the thread used to stitch them in place remains visible. When you use the washer/nut method, a small bead not only holds the sequin in place, but it also hides the thread!

Begin with the lock stitch. Pass the threaded needle through the hole of the sequin, then add a small seed bead. Draw the sequin down to the fabric surface, and pass the needle through the sequin's hole to the wrong side of the fabric, bypassing the small bead. Finish on the back with a tie-off knot. The seed bead sits over the hole, giving the embellishment a lovely finish.

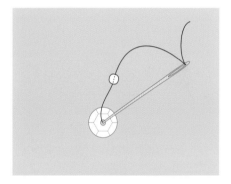

Washer/Nut Method
Sequin

DAIRY CHRISTMAS *(detail) by Mary Stori. I used the washer/nut method to create the bovines' sequin eyes and the starry snowflakes. For a full view of the quilt, see page 65.*

Charms and Trinkets

Untidy threads are a thing of the past! You can sew charms and other trinkets to your quilts with the basic washer/nut method as described on page 21. Be sure your "nut" bead is larger than the hole of the charm or trinket you have selected.

Larger charms or trinkets may have more than one hole, but that's no problem. Just repeat, adding a bead to cover each hole.

Washer/Nut Method
Charms and trinkets

TROPICAL FISH STICKS *(detail) by Mary Stori.*
An example of attaching charms and trinkets. The small brass starfish charm acts as the "washer," while a small gold seed bead "nut" secures it to the quilt. For a full view of the quilt, see page 81.

Buttons

Now that you are beading, why sew on buttons with just ordinary thread? In fact, why not use buttons to embellish and add interest to your quilts, with the button as the "washer" and the attaching beads as the "nuts"? Here are a few ideas to get you started, but please don't be limited to just these suggestions. Feel free to play and come up with your own ideas.

If you intend to use these buttons as functional closures, I'd recommend passing the thread through twice.

Attaching a Two-Hole Button

Attaching a two-hole button is just like using the washer/nut method to attach a sequin, except the button has two holes. Position the button on the fabric. Begin with a lock stitch directly below one of the buttonholes, bringing the needle up through that hole to the right side of the fabric. String a seed bead onto the thread, and pass the needle back through the same buttonhole, drawing the thread to the wrong side of the fabric so that the bead covers the hole. Travel on the wrong side of the fabric to the opposite hole, and repeat, eliminating the lock stitch. Finish with a tie-off knot on the fabric's wrong side.

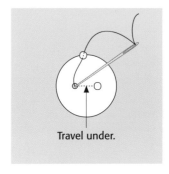

Travel under.

Washer/Nut Method
Two-hole button

HERE COME THE HYBRIDS *(detail) by Mary Stori.*
An example of attaching buttons. The eyes of the cauliflower
were made by beading one seed bead in each hole of the star
buttons. For a full view of quilt, see page 42.

Attaching a Four-Hole Button

You can attach a four-hole button even when the attaching beads are slightly smaller than the button's hole, but you'll need to use more beads.

Position the button on the fabric. Execute the lock stitch directly below one of the buttonholes, bringing the needle up through that hole to the right side of the fabric. Add enough seed beads to completely cover the thread when the needle is reinserted into the *diagonally* opposite hole. This number will vary, of course, according to the size of the beads and the distance between buttonholes. I usually try three or four beads to start.

Repeat to cover the thread spanning the remaining two holes, keeping in mind that you'll probably need one or two additional beads for the second "string" to accommodate the extra thread it requires to cross the first. Finish with a tie-off knot.

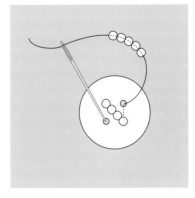

Washer/Nut Method
Four-hole button

Another method for attaching a four-hole button involves combining different types of beads, such as seed and bugle beads.

Position the button on the fabric. Execute the lock stitch directly below one of the buttonholes, bringing the needle up through that hole to the right side of the fabric. String one seed bead, one small bugle bead—size #1 is usually about right—and a second seed bead onto the thread. Pass the needle through the opposite hole to the wrong side of the fabric. The goal is to have each seed bead sit over a hole, with the bugle bead spanning the distance between.

Run the thread along the wrong side of the fabric, emerging at one of the two remaining holes. Span the final two holes by repeating the same bead sequence, and use the tie-off knot to finish.

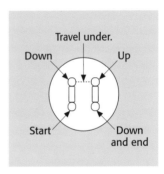

Washer/Nut Method
Four-hole button

Sometimes adjustments must be made
to obtain the correct spacing between
buttonholes. Consider using larger seed
beads—or even two seed beads instead
of one—over each hole.

Or try this: Position the button on the fabric. Execute the lock stitch directly below one of the buttonholes, bringing the needle up through that hole to the right side of the fabric. Working clockwise, add enough seed beads to completely cover the thread when the needle is reinserted into the next hole, plus two additional beads. Insert the needle into the next hole and bring it to the right side of the fabric through the same hole. Continue in this manner for all four holes. Finish with a tie-off knot. The strings of beads are slightly loopy, which suggests the outline of a flower. Have fun: experiment by changing bead colors, or by adding a second round of beads.

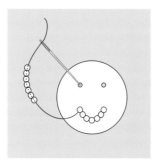

Washer/Nut Method
Four-hole button

Shanks

I dread making buttonholes on my garments! Instead, I prefer to use loops made from fabric, cord, or ribbon, and enjoy featuring distinctive beads, rather than buttons, as fasteners. Here's a nifty trick I developed when I realized that sometimes the washer/nut method held the bead to the fabric too tightly and did not allow enough room for the loop to serve its purpose: add an extra bead underneath the "featured" bead to act as a shank, providing space to accommodate the loop.

Begin with a lock stitch at the point where the button will be placed, and bring the threaded needle through to the right side of the fabric. String a seed bead, the larger "featured" bead, and another seed bead onto the thread. Pass the needle back through the featured bead, the initial seed bead, and the fabric. Run the thread through a second time, and finish by pulling tightly on the thread and securing a tie-off knot.

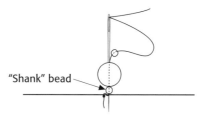

"Shank" bead

The size of the "shank" bead may change depending upon the size of the hole in the featured bead and/or the diameter of the fabric loop. You'll need to keep these factors in mind when creating shank button closures.

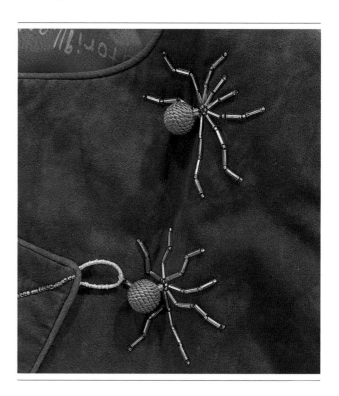

Spinning around the Web *(vest detail) by Mary Stori. An example of creating a shank. A small pearl was used as the "spacer" shank beneath the corded bead "button" (spider body) to accommodate the thick cord loops.*

MAKING DANGLES

DANGLES TECHNIQUES have so many possibilities, they could easily fill a complete chapter!

I work with a size #11 or #12 Sharp when I am making dangles. Because it is long and thin, I'm less likely to have difficulties reinserting the threaded needle through beads that already contain thread.

Let's explore four different methods to make dangles.

The first method is similar to the washer/nut method, but with one big difference. Instead of the featured item (such as a charm) acting as the "washer," it now becomes the "nut." Begin with a lock stitch at the point where you want the embellishment to be placed, bringing the threaded needle up to the right side of the fabric. String seven seed beads and the embellishment onto the thread. Pass the threaded needle back through all seven seed beads, reinserting it into the fabric right next to the spot where it first emerged. Be very careful as you pass back through the beads so as not to split and weaken the thread. Finish with a tie-off knot.

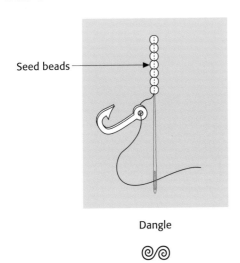

Seed beads

Dangle

Seven is just a suggested number of beads to use for this technique; you can use as many as you like. However, stick with an uneven number. That seems to work best.

Beads dangling on a thread can enhance other design elements. Each time I've traveled as an instructor on Specialty Tour's Quilting Cruises, I've made commemorative cruise pins for my students. The example shown on page 27 illustrates how effective a few well-placed beads can be.

This technique isn't restricted to three-dimensional fabric surfaces. Consider adding beads to your next pieced or appliquéd quilt that features flower motifs. Begin with a lock stitch, emerging with the threaded needle in the center of the flower. String one round bead (approximately 4 mm) and twenty-one seed beads in any color combination you wish. Pass the threaded needle back through the first six seed beads strung, the round bead, and the background fabric, pulling the thread snug on the fabric's wrong side. Bring the needle back to the front side of the fabric, through the large bead, avoiding the previously beaded threads. Repeat the stringing procedure with the same sequence of beads, or change the look by altering the number of beads and/or the point at which you reenter the line of beads.

Always finish by pulling the thread tight on the wrong side of the fabric. Complete with a secure tie-off knot at the end of the entire sequence.

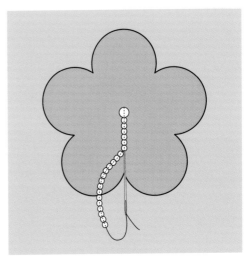

Dangle
Flower stamen

Here's another simple loop dangle that has many possibilities beyond flower stamens. Once again, the character of the decoration can easily be changed by varying the number, size, and colors of the beads. I like to make at least two loops, working one loop through the other and using a base bead to provide support.

Begin with a lock stitch, emerging with the threaded needle in the center of the flower, or any other desired spot on the fabric surface. String one round bead (approximately 4 mm) and seventeen seed beads in any color combination you wish. Pass the threaded needle back through the large bead and the background fabric, pulling the thread snug on the fabric's wrong side. Bring the needle back to the front side of the fabric, avoiding the previously beaded thread. Pass it through the large bead and add thirteen seed beads. Bring the needle through the first loop so that one loop passes beneath the other. Pass the needle through the large bead and background fabric, pull tightly on the thread, and tie off with a knot on the back.

The final example is slightly more elaborate and—of course—has many applications besides the "hair ornament" you see pictured on page 27. Note that it doesn't matter whether you stitch from right to left or left to right for this technique.

Begin with a lock stitch, emerging with the threaded needle at the point you want one of the bead lines to begin. String seven same-colored seed beads, one seed bead in a contrasting color, one "gem" (or larger decorative bead), and one seed bead in the same contrasting color as the other "oddball" seed bead. Pass the threaded needle back through the "gem" and the second contrasting seed bead. Add seven more seed beads in the same color as the first seven strung. Pass the needle through the background fabric, pull tightly on the thread, and tie off with a knot on the back.

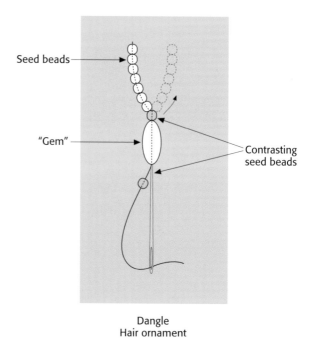

Dangle
Hair ornament

Dangle
Bead loops

ISLAND HOPPING #1 *(detail) by Mary Stori.*
An example of dangles. A string of seed beads is used to attach
and give movement to the fishhook charm.

SUNSHINE IN MY GARDEN *(detail) by Mary Stori.*
Two loop dangles are intertwined to create the flower stamen.
The beadwork also holds the silk flower to the quilt.
For a full view of the quilt, see page 90.

Commemorative cruise pin by Mary Stori, 1999.
Seed-bead dangles become whimsical stamens for this flower.

THE GODDESS OF QUILTING *(detail) by Mary Stori.*
The hair-ornament dangle features a decorative bead
suspended between two strings of beads. For a full view
of the quilt, see page 46.

Securing Miscellaneous Embellishments with Beads

Attaching miscellaneous, or "found," objects can present a challenge. Generally, I find that as long as the item isn't too bulky or heavy, it should work!

If a treasure you wish to add doesn't have a hole, you can make one. Often a tiny drill bit fixed to my Dremel tool is the answer for me. Holes can also be melted through plastic objects with a straight pin (for flimsier items) or a metal skewer (for more substantial items) that has been heated over the flame of a butane lighter or gas stove. Don't forget to protect your fingers!

Once you've made a hole, treat the item like a button, using seed beads to cover the holes and hide the thread. Let's look at some examples.

Each time I teach on a cruise, I can't wait to create new projects and techniques for students to learn. Passengers don't use cash aboard ship; instead each is issued a special credit card for purchases. You can use this method to attach any card to your quilt. Here's how it's done.

Drill holes in all four corners of the card.

Thread the needle with a long length of thread (about 24"), knotting the thread tail. Bring the threaded needle up from the wrong side of the fabric, through one of the pre-drilled holes. String one seed bead (larger than the hole) onto the thread, and reinsert the needle through the hole in the card and the background fabric. Travel on the wrong side of the fabric to the next hole, repeating the procedure until each of the four corners is secured with a seed bead. Finish with a tie-off knot.

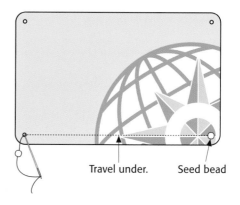

Travel under.   Seed bead

I melted holes through doll shoes for "Along the Quilting Highway" (detail below). I attached them in the same manner as a two-hole button (see page 22). A teaching trip to New Mexico inspired this quilt. I won't even try to explain it; you just had to be there!

ISLAND HOPPING #2 *(detail) by Mary Stori.*
After drilling a small hole in each corner of the plastic credit card, I used a seed bead to hide the thread and secure the embellishment. For a full view of the quilt, see page 43.

ALONG THE QUILTING HIGHWAY *(detail) by Mary Stori.*
I used a hot skewer to melt holes in the plastic shoes. Seed beads cover the thread that holds them on the quilt. For a full view of the quilt, see page 44.

The miniature plastic champagne glass I chose for "Party Animals" (quilt on page 45) already had a hole. However, when I tried to attach it with the washer/nut method, it stuck out at an odd angle. To solve the problem, I ran a string of beads through the hole, making it into a loop to hold the glass onto the quilt and provide some movement, much like a dangle.

To re-create this method, start with a lock stitch, emerging with the threaded needle at the spot where you wish the embellishment to be placed. String enough seed beads onto the thread to form a loop large enough for the object to lie properly on the quilt when the loop is secured. For this method, the beads need to be *smaller* than the hole so they can slide through it.

When you are satisfied with the length of the loop, pass the threaded needle back through the first bead strung, reinserting it into the fabric right next to the spot where it first emerged. Finish with a tie-off knot.

The same washer/nut method used to attach sequins (see page 21) can be utilized to attach other single-hole items. No need to resort to glues or live with visible messy threads. Some objects, such as the old watch faces in "Brain Cramps" (detail below), may have sharp edges that can damage the quilt. Use a metal file, steel wool, sandpaper, a wire cutter, or even pliers to pinch areas flat and eliminate rough edges.

BRAIN CRAMPS *(detail) by Mary Stori.*
Watch faces are stitched to the quilt with the aid of a seed bead. For a full view of the quilt, see page 71.

BEAD APPLIQUÉ

BEAD APPLIQUÉ IS a timesaving technique that permits you to embellish and appliqué in one step. This method uses beads to "tack down" the appliqué design, rather than the traditional method of flat appliqué followed by embellishment.

Bead appliqué is most appropriate when the edges of the appliqué are finished or don't require finishing. The edges of appliqués cut from Ultra Suede or felt, for example, will not fray, nor will silk or ribbon flowers or leaves. I hope the examples provided kick your creativity up a notch or two!

Twisted Ribbon

Cut a piece of ribbon about twice the desired finished length. Begin with a lock stitch at the point where you wish the ribbon appliqué to start, and bring the threaded needle to the right side of the fabric. Position the ribbon and bring the threaded needle up through its center, about ⅛" to ¼" from its starting end. String one seed bead, then draw the ribbon down to the quilt top. Reinsert the threaded needle into the ribbon and background fabric; use the basic bead stitch and pull the thread snug. The bead will hold the ribbon in place.

Twist the ribbon one or two times and hold it to the background fabric with your finger or thumb. Using the scatter-stitch method (see page 20), travel with the threaded needle 1" to 2" on the wrong side of the fabric, emerging through both fabric and ribbon right next to your finger. Add another bead, and then stitch through both the ribbon and the background fabric. Continue in this manner until you have reached a point about ⅛" to ¼" from the far end of the ribbon, and finish with a tie-off knot on the wrong side of the fabric. The ribbon/bead appliqué techynique may be enhanced by twisting several ribbons together before stitching.

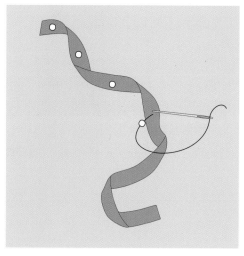

Bead Appliqué

Three-Dimensional Appliqué

As with bead appliqué, three-dimensional appliqué yields its best results if you use an appliqué with finished edges. Position the appliqué on the quilt top. Use the scatter-stitch method (see page 20) to stitch through all fabric layers, attaching the appliqué with any combination of bead shapes you wish. If you are adding the appliqué to a completed quilt and wish to avoid messy threads showing on the quilt back, pass the needle through the top two layers only.

SUNSHINE IN MY GARDEN *(detail) by Mary Stori. I used the scatter-stitch technique to bead appliqué these silk leaves in place. For a full view of the quilt, see page 90.*

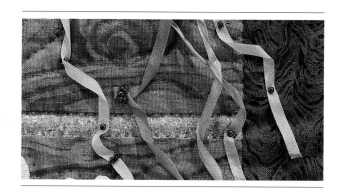

PARTY ANIMALS *(detail) by Mary Stori. I created party streamers by attaching a single twisted silk ribbon to the quilt with beads. For a full view of the quilt, see page 45.*

DECORATIVE STITCHES

SOME OF THE names and styles of the following decorative stitches may look familiar to you if you do embroidery. Again, these ideas are just a sampling of the embellishing options possible.

You may work with a longer thread for these techniques to avoid constant tying-off and rethreading. If noticeable fraying or frustrating twisting occurs, simply tie off and begin again with a shorter thread length. Study each method before you begin; you'll probably find that an appliqué needle works best for stringing multiple beads and passing back through beads that have already been strung. Take care that you don't split the thread as you pass back through the beads. This can cause the thread to weaken, break, or get snarled up inside a bead.

Daisy Stitch

Begin with a lock stitch, bringing the threaded needle to the right side of the fabric where you wish to place the design. String ten seed beads onto the thread. Pass the threaded needle back through the first bead strung. Add one seed bead in a different color—and slightly larger, if you like—and pass the needle back through the fifth bead strung. Pull the beaded thread to flip the large bead to the center and form a "flower head," and secure by reinserting the threaded needle into the background fabric. Finish with a tie-off knot on the fabric's wrong side.

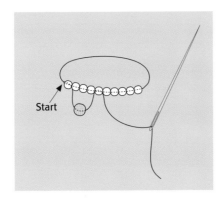

Daisy Stitch

If you are repeating a beaded daisy stitch and traveling more than 2" under the background fabric, it is best to tie off after each flower to maintain the proper thread tension.

THE GODDESS OF QUILTING *(detail) by Mary Stori.*
The daisy stitch creates the flowers on the pillar.
For a full view of the quilt, see page 46.

Chain Stitch

Begin with a lock stitch, bringing the threaded needle to the right side of the fabric where you wish to place the design. String thirteen seed beads onto the thread. Pass the threaded needle back through the first two beads strung and into the background fabric. Travel under the background fabric, and bring the needle back to the right side of the fabric, reemerging inside the far edge of the previous circle. Add another thirteen seed beads and repeat. To end the chain, bring the needle up inside the final beaded circle and add two seed beads. Reinsert the needle into the background fabric just outside the final circle, and tie off with a knot on the fabric's wrong side.

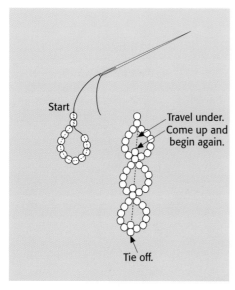

Chain Stitch

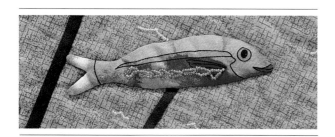

TROPICAL FISH STICKS *(detail) by Mary Stori.*
I used the chain stitch to decorate this stuffed fish motif
with color-lined beads that resemble fish scales.
For a full view of the quilt, see page 81.

Picot Stitch

Begin with a lock stitch, bringing the threaded needle to the right side of the fabric where you wish to place the design. String an uneven number of seed beads onto the thread. Using the basic bead stitch (see page 15), back up and reinsert the needle into the fabric about two bead lengths short of the threaded length of beads. Because the distance spanned by the thread is actually shorter than the length of threaded beads, the beads pop up in a hump.

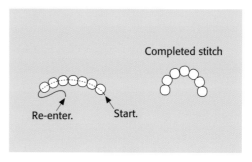

Picot stitch

The picot stitch can be worked as an individual motif, a series of individual motifs, or in rows. When you sew rows, you must bring up the threaded needle on the six o'clock side of the first strung bead, spanning the same distance as the space between the first and last bead of the "hump." By varying the number of beads and the distance the thread travels, you can alter the look and application of this embellishment.

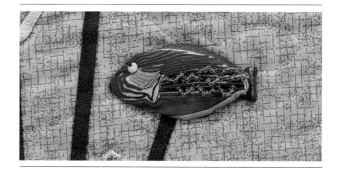

TROPICAL FISH STICKS *(detail) by Mary Stori.*
Three-cut glass beads in rows of picot stitch embellish the fish
design. For a full view of the quilt, see page 81.

WAVES

THE WAVE TECHNIQUE is easier to accomplish if you use a removable marking tool to draw a "wave" line to follow and stitch in the direction indicated in the diagram below. Begin with a lock stitch, bringing the threaded needle to the right side of the fabric at the beginning of the line. Use the basic bead stitch to follow the marked line, attaching the beads as usual. When you reach the top of the wave, bring the needle up *below* the bead, one bead length away. This shift in direction allows the next wave section to "fall" correctly as you continue with the basic bead stitch.

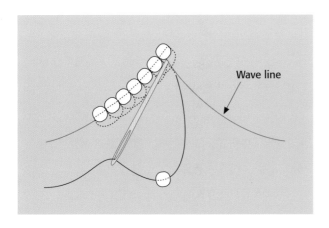

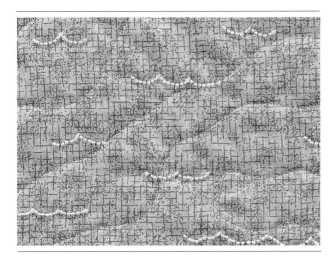

THE GODDESS OF QUILTING *(detail) by Mary Stori.*
Seed-bead waves help to identify this turquoise background
as water rather than sky. For a full view of the quilt,
see page 46.

BUGLE-BEAD WALL

THE BUGLE-BEAD wall is another decorative textural technique with many applications.

Begin with a lock stitch, bringing the threaded needle through to the right side of the fabric where the wall is to begin. String two bugle beads onto the thread, standing them upright, side by side on the fabric. Reinsert the threaded needle through the fabric, directly under the second bead. Bring the threaded needle back to the right side of the fabric, just beside the second bead. String one bugle bead; then pass the needle once again through the second bead and background fabric. Continue adding beads, each time reinserting the threaded needle through the previous bead and background fabric, until you have stitched the desired design.

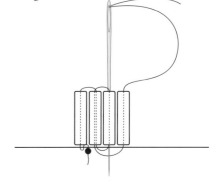

Bugle-Bead Wall

STANDING TALL FOR THE RED, WHITE, & BLUE
(detail) by Mary Stori. An example of a bugle-bead wall.
For a full view of the quilt, see page 53.

Bugle-Bead Twisted Wall

To make this variation, follow the instructions for the bugle-bead wall on page 33. After the design is completely stitched, gently lay a section of beaded wall down flat on the fabric. Knot a length of thread and, entering from the back side, beneath the flattened area of beadwork, bring the threaded needle up to the right side of the fabric. Take a tiny stitch between two of the bugle beads, crossing the thread between them, and pass the needle back to the wrong side of the fabric. For added strength, stitch a second time.

Bend the beaded wall in the opposite direction, and repeat the tacking stitch. Continue as desired.

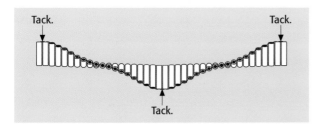

Bugle-Bead Twisted Wall

Tropical Fish Sticks *(detail) by Mary Stori.*
A variation of the bugle-bead wall is created by folding and tacking beaded sections onto the fabric, giving the appearance of a twisted line. For a full view of the quilt, see page 81.

Spikes

I like to create this standing bugle/seed bead combination in units of three "spikes" or more. It makes a great flower center (see "Sunshine in My Garden" on page 90). Working them through a large bead provides additional support, helping to keep the spikes upright. With the exception of the support bead, sizes and colors are determined more by your project than the mechanics of the stitch. There is no "wrong" way to sew this technique, so have fun coming up with your own bead mixtures.

Begin with a lock stitch, bringing the threaded needle through to the right side of the fabric where you wish to position the embellishment. String one large round bead (a size #5 or #6), then alternate a seed bead, a bugle bead, a seed, a bugle, and a seed. Bypassing the last seed bead, pass the threaded needle back through the final bugle, the other remaining beads on the thread (including the large "support" bead), and the background fabric. Pull the thread tight.

To make additional spikes, bring the threaded needle up through the fabric, a thread or two of the fabric weave from the previous spike. Pass the needle through the same large bead and repeat the combination of seed and bugle beads and the stitching order—or create a new one as shown in the illustration below. Be sure to pull the thread tight on the back after completing each spike.

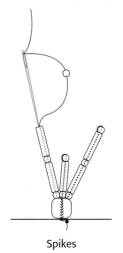

Spikes

TRIM

BEADED EMBELLISHMENT ALONG the seam line of your quilt or garment binding adds a nice finishing touch (see "German Goose-Feather Tree" on page 86). The type and number of beads can be adapted to complement the project design and size. Beading is done after the quilt is quilted and bound, so make every effort to keep the stitches hidden underneath the binding.

Working on one side of the quilt at a time, mark reference points every inch along the binding with straight pins. Knot a length of thread, and slide the threaded needle under the binding on the back of the quilt near a corner to bury the knot. Bring the needle up at the corner on the right side of the quilt. String thirteen three-cut beads (size #9) and six seed beads (size #10 or #11) onto the thread. Pass the needle back through the last three-cut bead strung, and pull the thread to gather the seed beads. This beaded unit should end exactly at the first 1" marker. Take a tiny stitch under the binding, and bring the needle back to the right side of the quilt, along the seam line of the binding and close to the previous ending stitch. Continue making these units until you've gone completely around the perimeter of the quilt.

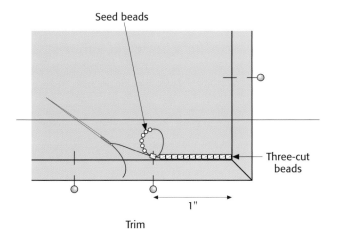

Trim

BEAD NET

THE BEAD-NET technique is often used in jewelry making, and there are countless bead combinations to explore. Use a #11 or #12 Sharp needle and long lengths of thread (about 36") for this technique, and keep the thread tension tight as you work. The longer thread lengths mean you don't have to add more thread before the net is finished.

To introduce you to the basic technique, let's learn how to make a small 2½"-wide net. As you can see from the detail of "Tropical Fish Sticks" (see page 36), I beaded a total of four rows and turned mine into a fishing net, but you can make as many rows as desired. The "netting" doesn't appear square because I bunched it over a fish charm before tacking it to the quilt. One normally leaves the lower edge and sides of bead nets free and loose, but they can also be sewn directly onto the fabric surface or used as insets to join fabric pieces together.

Use the steps that follow to practice beading a net. Use size #10 seed beads and size #3 twisted bugle beads.

1. Draw a 2"-long line on the fabric, with reference marks indicated at every half-inch. Begin with a lock stitch, and use the basic bead stitch to sew a seed bead at each mark, finishing with a tie-off knot at the end of the line.

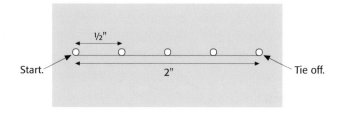

2. Beginning on the wrong side with a new knotted thread, bring the needle up through both the fabric and the first bead. String 1 bugle bead, 1 seed bead, and 1 bugle bead onto the thread, angling them as shown in the diagram below. Pass the threaded needle back through the second seed bead. Do not catch the background fabric.

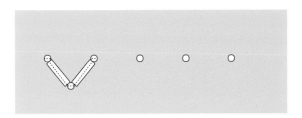

3. Repeat this sequence to complete the row, each time passing through the last seed bead but not the fabric. When you reach the end of the line, add a bugle bead, a seed bead, a bugle bead, a seed bead, and a bugle before passing through the final seed bead in the second row. Keep the thread tension tight.

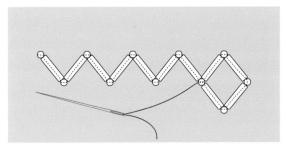

Bead Net

4. You've now changed direction! Repeat the bead sequence described in steps 2 and 3, reversing directions at the end of each row until you have added the desired rows.

Here's how to extend your beading thread when you want to continue with a line of netting or fringe.

Stop beading with at least six inches of thread left on the needle. This allows you room to manipulate the beading. Tie a new length of thread to the old with a square knot. If you are unsure of your ability to form a secure knot, put a speck of clear fingernail polish on the knot, let it dry, trim the thread ends, and proceed with your stitching.

TROPICAL FISH STICKS *(detail) by Mary Stori.*
Bugle and seed beads combine to create a fishnet.
For a full view of the quilt, see page 81.

FRINGE

FRINGE CONSISTS OF individual strands or strings of beads worked side by side. It's great when attached to the top or bottom edge of a quilt, and can really dress up a garment, too! Use the technique and its many variations however you see fit.

Beaded fringe can be worked in such diverse patterns that once you have a basic understanding of the technique, you'll be able to create combinations of sizes and shapes that suit your pieces best. Use an appliqué needle (#11 or #12 Sharp) and long lengths of thread (about 36"), and keep the thread tension tight as you work.

NOTE: *Strands of fringe can also be worked in units, with the bottom edge of the fringe connecting with the next strand or row. I classify these multiple rows of fringe as netting, although others may still call them fringe.*

Fringe Trim

Here's one of my favorites! You'll be starting in a corner of the quilt and working in the direction shown in the illustration at right. The beading sequence can be repeated over and over to achieve the desired measurement. Bead sizes shown here are suggested—but not required—sizes.

Determine where and how long you want the strand of fringe to run, and mark reference points at 1" intervals, including the beginning and ending of the line. Begin with a lock stitch, bringing the threaded needle up where you want the line of fringe to start. String one seed bead (size #8), four bugle beads (size #1 or #2), one seed bead (size #11), one decorative bead (seed or otherwise, size #7 or larger), and seven seed beads (size #11) onto the thread. Pass the threaded needle back through the decorative bead only, and add one seed bead (size #11), four bugle beads (size #1 or #2), and one seed bead (size #8). Reenter the fabric at the

second 1" reference mark. Bring the needle back to the right side of the fabric, passing through the last seed bead strung. The resulting small stitch is hidden beneath the binding on the back of the quilt. Repeat the stringing and stitching sequence until the fringe has reached the desired length, and finish with a tie-off knot hidden inside the binding.

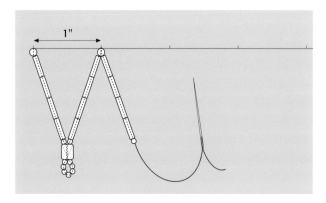

Fringe Trim

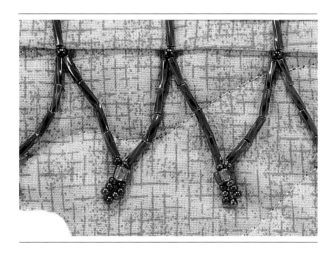

THE GODDESS OF QUILTING *(detail) by Mary Stori.*
The bead fringe adds an exotic feel to this project.
For a full view of the quilt, see page 46.

Branched Fringe

Work branched fringe as a single "string" or in a row. Either way, it's lots of fun to do. Beading identical fringes is not important; in fact, the look is more appealing when you vary the beading sequence. The "branches" can grow out of the central string where and how they look best. Use a size #11 or #12 Sharp and—if beading in a row—a long length of thread.

Begin with a lock stitch, bringing the threaded needle up where you want the fringe to start. String eleven seed beads, and then pass the needle back through the *next-to-last bead strung*, pulling the thread completely through. String a few more seed beads; let's say four. Reenter the next-to-last bead strung on this "branch," passing the threaded needle back through the remaining three beads and reentering the central "string" again.

Run the threaded needle back up through a few more beads, and exit where you want the next branch to be. Gently pull the thread tight after each branch is created. Continue moving up the fringe until you reach the top. Bring the needle through to the wrong side of the fabric, and either tie off with a knot or travel to where the next fringe begins.

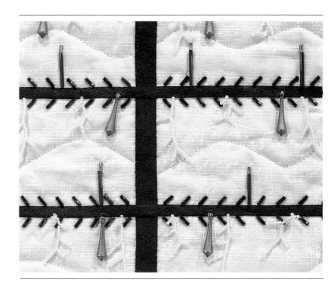

GERMAN GOOSE-FEATHER TREE *(detail) by Mary Stori.*
Branched fringe is worked as single units along a row.
For a full view of the quilt, see page 86.

SUNSHINE IN MY GARDEN *(detail) by Mary Stori.*
Flower stamens are created by making several
branched fringe "strings" in the center of one flower.
For a full view of the quilt, see page 90.

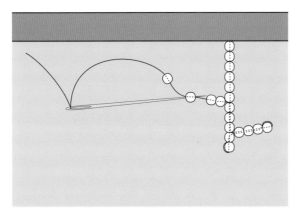

Branched Fringe

Sewing Skills

*T*HIS BOOK IS not intended as a how-to resource for basic quiltmaking techniques. There are lots of good ones out there, and I encourage you to refer to them as necessary. That said, I am including some instructions for a few specific techniques that recur throughout the directions for the projects in this book.

Hand Appliqué

THIS TECHNIQUE IS used to sew one piece of fabric on top of another.

Appliqués Cut from Woven Fabric

To achieve tidy edges when working with appliqués cut from woven fabrics (such as cotton), use a washable or erasable marking tool to trace the finished size of the appliqué motif onto the right side of the fabric. Add a scant ¼"-wide seam allowance when cutting out the fabric shape. Fold the seam allowance to the wrong side of the appliqué and finger press it in place using the marked line as a guide.

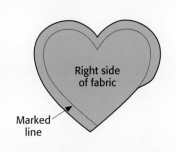

For pucker-free appliqué, cut the appliqué motif and the background fabric so that the grain lines run in the same direction.

When using Ultra Suede or craft felt, it's not necessary to match the grain line of the appliqué to the quilt.

Position the prepared appliqué, and pin or thread baste it in place. Thread an appliqué needle, often referred to as a Sharp or Straw needle, with thread that matches the appliqué fabric. Use a blind stitch to secure the appliqué to the background fabric, catching only a thread or two of the appliqué motif, just beneath the fold.

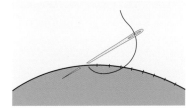

Appliqué Stitch

Appliqués Cut from Specialty Fabrics

Because their edges do not fray, some specialty fabrics, such as Ultra Suede and craft felt, can be appliquéd without the need to turn under a seam allowance. I love working with these materials because appliqué designs can be cut their exact finished size, and the stitching process is hassle free! For wonderful results, blindstitch right along the fabric edge, using a long, thin appliqué needle and thread to match the appliqué fabric.

EMBROIDERY

A FEW PROJECTS in this book call for the outline stitch to enhance the pieced, appliquéd, or embellished design. The outline stitch creates a continuous, slightly textured line, which can be used to punctuate and draw attention to many design elements. The results will vary depending upon the number of strands of embroidery floss used and the length of the stitches. Always secure the fabric in a hoop when working the outline stitch.

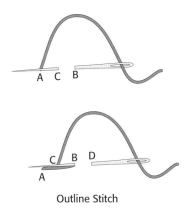

Outline Stitch

BINDING

1. Trim the backing and batting even with the raw edges of the quilt top.

   NOTE: *If you have cut the quilt top oversized to fit in a frame for beading, trim the entire sandwich to the finished measurement as indicated in the project instructions.*

2. Determine the total length of the binding required by measuring the length and width of the quilt, adding the measurements together, and multiplying by 2. Add an extra 10" for seams, corner turns, and overlap at the starting point.

3. Cut enough 2¼"-wide strips from the crosswise grain of the binding fabric to equal the measurement you figured in step 2. Piece the strips together end to end, joining them with a right-angled seam. Press the seams open.

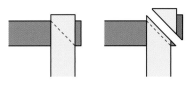

Joining Straight-Cut Strips

4. Mark and trim one end of the binding strip at a 45° angle. Fold a ¼"-wide seam allowance to the wrong side and press.

5. Fold the binding strip in half lengthwise, wrong sides together, and press.

6. With right sides together, and starting with the binding's angled end, line up the long raw edge of the binding strip with the raw edge of the quilt. Leave the first 3" of the binding loose, and begin machine stitching the binding to the quilt. Use a ¼"-wide seam, and a walking foot if you have one.

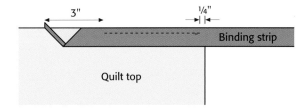

7. Stop stitching ¼" from the first corner of the quilt. Make 1 stitch in place, raise the needle and presser foot, and turn the quilt so you will be ready to stitch down the next edge. Fold the binding up, away from the quilt, with raw

edges aligned. A 45°-angle fold will appear at the corner. Hold the fold in place as you fold the strip back down onto itself, even with the edge of the quilt top. The fold at the top edge of the binding should be even with the top edge of the quilt.

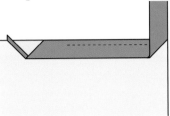

8. Resume stitching at the top edge of the quilt, and repeat the process for the remaining corners.

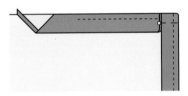

9. As you approach the beginning of the binding, stop and make a few stitches in place. Raise the presser foot and needle, and overlap the starting edge of the binding by an inch or two. Cut away any excess binding, trimming it at a 45° angle. Slip the cut end of the binding strip into the starting fold and finish the seam.

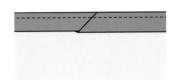

10. Fold the binding over the raw edge to the back of the quilt. The folded edge of the binding should cover the stitching line. Blindstitch the binding to the quilt, catching the backing fabric only.

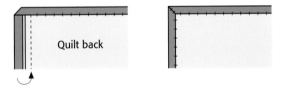

Quilt back

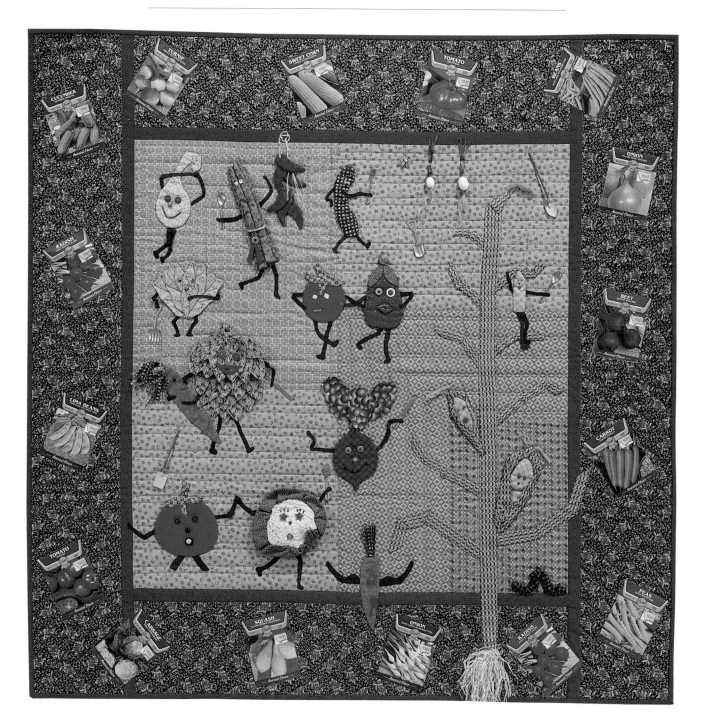

HERE COME THE HYBRIDS

by Mary Stori, 1996, Brodhead, Wisconsin, 45" x 45".

☙

An invitation to make a quilt for a traveling exhibit gave me the idea for this machine-pieced, hand-appliquéd, hand-quilted, and embellished quilt. It was created all in good fun as a spoof of the exhibit's name: Enchanted Gardens!

BACON & EGGS

(LEFT)

BACON & EGGS
by Mary Stori, 1994,
Brodhead, Wisconsin, 50" x 55".

❧

I have fun creating quilts based on
word play. This hand-appliquéd,
hand-quilted piece features stuffed
pigs and chickens. Beads are used
to create eggs in a basket,
yellow chicken feed, and ears of corn.

(RIGHT)

ISLAND HOPPING #2
by Mary Stori, 1997, Brodhead,
Wisconsin, 21½" x 20".

❧

I designed this whimsical quilt
to teach embellishment techniques
on a western Caribbean quilting
cruise. Beaded lines denote
the itinerary of the ship,
while the appliquéd islands
feature "tacky tourist mementos"
that have been beaded
to the quilt.

(LEFT)

ALONG THE QUILTING HIGHWAY
by Mary Stori, 1997, Brodhead, Wisconsin,
17" x 17".

೨೮

This quilt was inspired by a
display of boots and shoes on
wooden guardrail posts along a highway near
Los Alamos, New Mexico. The plastic doll
shoes are attached with seed beads.

(RIGHT)

SPRING GREEN
by Mary Stori, 1997, Brodhead, Wisconsin,
11" x 20".

೨೮

Woodland fiddlehead ferns were
my inspiration for this hand-stippled quilted
piece, which features trapunto work. The tiny
scatter-stitched beads resemble dewdrops.

(LEFT)

PARTY ANIMALS
*by Mary Stori, 1996, Brodhead,
Wisconsin, 46" x 46".*

◎◎

*Most Wisconsin natives are familiar
with the "trophies" that adorn the walls of
weekend cabins and cottages. I suspect
that when the homeowners are away,
the animals come to life and
have their own parties.*

(RIGHT)

TECHNOLOGY GONE BERSERK
*by Mary Stori, 1996, Brodhead,
Wisconsin, 53" x 58".*

◎◎

*This hand-appliquéd, hand-quilted
piece expresses my frustration over
automated telephone services that—
despite their announcements—have
not simplified our lives! Bead
embellishments depict eyes, earrings,
and telephone and clothing details.*

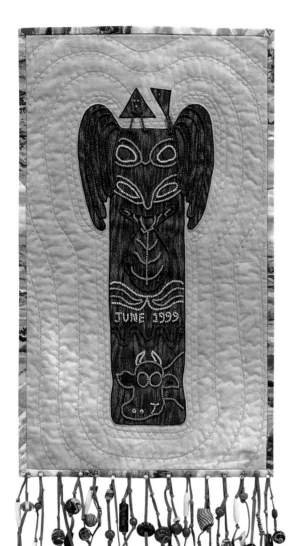

(LEFT)

TOTEM ART
*by Mary Stori, 1998, Brodhead, Wisconsin,
10½" x 18".*

☙

*An opportunity to teach on an Alaskan
quilting cruise led me to bead the design
I created for students to practice their
hand-quilting skills. Many quilt motifs can
be worked with straight or curved
beading techniques.*

(RIGHT)

THE GODDESS OF QUILTING
*by Mary Stori, 1999, Brodhead, Wisconsin,
13" x 17½".*

☙

*Designed by Mary Stori and
Sharee Dawn Roberts.
Sharee Dawn and I co-taught the beading
and embroidery techniques displayed on
this workshop project for my
1999 Greek Isles quilting cruise.*

(LEFT)

SNOWFLAKE

Mary Stori, 1997, Brodhead, Wisconsin,
9½" x 9".

The beaded snowflake was made of a
variety of silver-lined beads that sparkle
like sunlight on a fresh snowflake.

(RIGHT)

WAITING FOR SPRING

by Mary Stori, 1998, Brodhead,
Wisconsin, 30" x 30".

This quilt is a humorous look
at my husband, David,
sitting in his "toy" and wishing
winter were over!

PROJECTS

Now that you know just how easy it is to create beaded embellishments, I'm sure you're eager to begin a project. Each one presented here features one or more of the techniques illustrated in the previous chapter. Some can be executed faster than others, and all are great fun to create. I guarantee you'll be grabbing everything in sight, looking for embellishment possibilities!

Although I've attempted to be as specific as possible, calculating the number of beads required for a project is not an exact science. Therefore, I recommend purchasing extra beads, or at least checking to be sure additional beads are available if you should need them. The size of the beads indicated is also just a guideline. When a project calls for bugle beads, I've included the approximate length, which should make shopping easier since sizing can be so inconsistent.

You'll probably notice I often call for background fabric, batting, and/or backing to be cut larger than necessary. Sometimes this is to accommodate a hoop or frame, or to allow for the shrinkage that can occur during the quilting or embellishing process. In any case, you'll be instructed to trim the quilt sandwich down to size before the binding is added.

Now go have some fun!

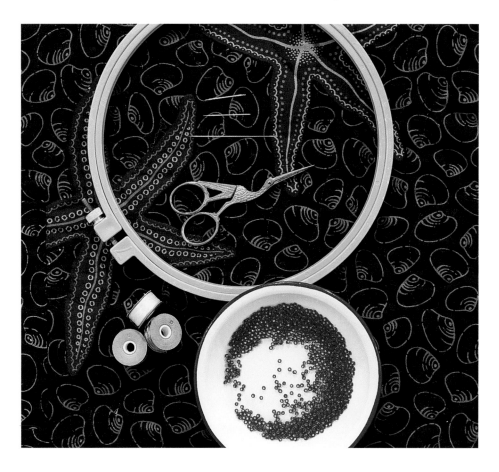

Caught in the Web *by Mary Stori, 1997, Brodhead, Wisconsin, 10" x 12".*
The spiderweb was created with quick curve beading, and features a dramatic beaded spider.

Here is an "immediate gratification" project to help you gain confidence while practicing your beading skills. Feel free to substitute fabric and bead colors to coordinate with your decor or personal preference.

☙☙

FINISHED QUILT SIZE: 10" X 12"

MATERIALS

42"-wide fabric

- 15" x 20" piece green mottled hand-dyed fabric for background
- 15" x 20" piece gold-and-green print fabric for backing
- 2 strips, each 2¼" x 42", gold mottled hand-dyed fabric for binding
- 15" x 20" piece thin, dense batting, such as Hobb's Thermore
- Black permanent pen
- Light box
- 425 gold twisted bugle beads, size 3*, for spiderweb
- 300 gold seed beads, size 10**, for spiderweb
- 50 black seed beads, size #11, for spider
- One ¼"- to ½"-long black oval decorative bead for spider body
- 1 black seed bead, size #5 or #6, for spider head
- 40 black bugle beads, size #2, for spider legs
- Nymo beading thread: gray or gold, and black
- Sewing thread to match binding fabric

* I used 2 tubes of TWE/BEADS item #3TB005 (see "Resources" on page 94).

** Available by the tube or hank to match bugle beads from TWE/BEADS.

BEADING THE QUILT

1. Fold the 15" x 20" green fabric in half vertically, horizontally, and diagonally to find the midpoint. Use a removable marker to center and mark a 9½" x 11½" rectangle on the right side of the creased green fabric. This outline marks the area that will contain the beaded design. You will add the seam allowance for the binding after the beadwork is completed.

2. Use a black permanent pen to trace the spiderweb pattern (page 52) onto white paper. Use a light box and a removable marker to transfer the design to the green fabric, keeping within the boundaries you marked in step 1.

3. Thread baste the batting to the wrong side of the marked quilt top in a 3" grid. The batting acts as a stabilizer for the weight of the beads and eliminates the need for quilting. You will now be treating the 2 layers as 1 layer.

4. Secure the 2-layered quilt sandwich in a hoop or frame. The oversized background fabric allows the entire piece to fit into a large hoop or 11" x 17" PVC-type quilting frame, which avoids the need for constant repositioning.

5. Bead the spiderweb design using the gold twisted bugle beads and gold seed beads and the quick curved method described and illustrated on page 18. Place a seed bead at each end of every bugle bead.

6. Create the spider's body using the picot technique described and illustrated on page 32. Begin with a lock stitch, bringing the threaded needle through to the right side of the fabric at the point where the "tail" end of the body will be. String 3 black seed beads (size #11), the large oval bead, 1 black seed bead (size #11), 1 black seed bead (size #5 or #6), and 1 black seed bead (size #11), onto the thread. Reinsert the needle into the background fabric, shortening the length of the stitch a little bit so the body pulls up slightly as described on page 32.

7. Bead 10 leg units, using a combination of 1 black seed bead (size #11), 1 black bugle bead, a black seed bead, a black bugle bead, a black seed bead, a black bugle bead, and another black seed bead for each leg. Once again, use the picot technique, shortening the length of the stitch and allowing the legs to "hump."

FINISHING

1. Remove the beaded quilt sandwich from the hoop or frame and carefully press the edges if needed. Be sure to keep steam away from the beads.

2. Layer the embellished 2-layer quilt sandwich (right side up) over the backing (wrong side up) on a clean, flat surface. Tape the corners to secure. Pin baste. Remove the tape.

3. Trim the entire quilt sandwich to measure 10" x 12", adjusting that figure to accommodate the beading if necessary.

4. Use the 2¼"-wide binding strips to bind the quilt as described in "Binding" on page 40.

Caught in the Web
Beading Pattern

STANDING TALL FOR
THE RED, WHITE, AND BLUE

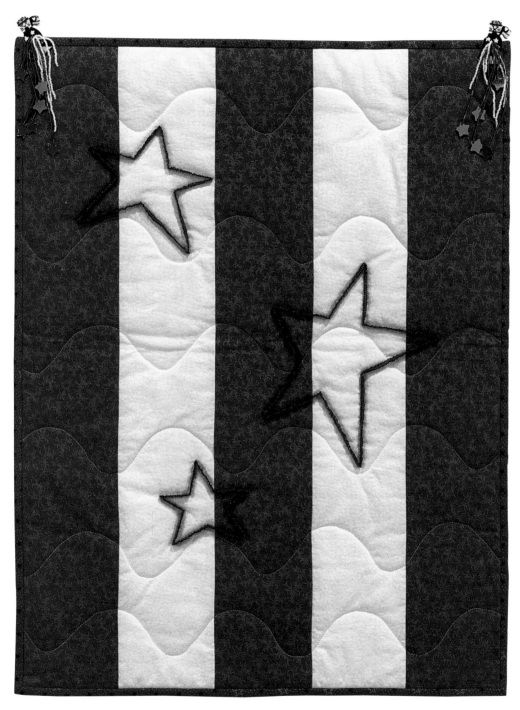

STANDING TALL FOR THE RED, WHITE, AND BLUE
by Mary Stori, 2000, Brodhead, Wisconsin, 20½" x 26".
Vivid blue bugle-bead stars and fun bead dangles are featured on this patriotic red-and-white strip-pieced wall quilt.

Let your patriotic spirit shine right along with the blue bugle-bead stars
as you make this simple, strip-pieced quilt.

☙☙

FINISHED QUILT SIZE: 20½" X 26"

MATERIALS

42"-wide fabric

- 1 yd. red fabric for pieced background and binding
- ⅞ yd. white fabric for pieced background and backing
- 22" x 28" piece of thin, dense batting, such as Hobb's Thermore or Hobb's 80/20 Heirloom
- Black permanent pen
- Light box
- 8 grams (approximately 1,400) blue bugle beads, ¼" long*, for stars
- 2 ceramic two-hole buttons in any design you choose for base of bead dangles
- 450–500 blue seed beads, size #10 or #11*, for dangles
- 12 blue glass stars** for dangles
- 300 white seed beads, size #10 or #11, for dangle loops
- Nymo beading thread: blue for the stars, blue and white for the dangles
- Sewing thread to match fabrics

* Mill Hill Beads, color Royal Blue to match glass stars. See "Resources" on page 94.

** Mill Hill Beads, item #12176, Royal Blue

CUTTING

NOTE: *To provide a sturdy foundation for the bead-work, cut fabric for this project on the lengthwise straight of grain.*

ALL MEASUREMENTS INCLUDE ¼"-wide seam allowances.

From the red fabric, cut:
- 3 strips, each 4½" x 26", for the pieced background
- 3 strips, each 2¼" x 36", for binding

From the white fabric, cut:
- 2 strips, each 4½" x 26", for the pieced background
- 1 piece, 22" x 28", for backing

PIECING THE BACKGROUND

SEW THE 4½" x 26" red and white strips together in the following order to make a strip set: red, white, red, white, red. Press seams toward the red strips.

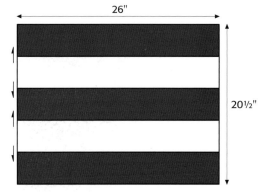

Embellishing the Quilt

1. Use a black permanent pen to trace star patterns A, B, and C (pages 56–57) onto white paper. With the aid of a light box, use a removable marking tool to trace the stars onto the quilt top. Refer to the quilt photo on page 53 and the diagram below for guidance.

Placement Diagram

2. To stabilize the project for the beading process, thread baste the batting to the wrong side of the marked quilt top. You will now be treating these 2 layers as 1 layer.

3. Refer to the bugle-bead wall technique described and illustrated on page 33, and use the ¼" blue bugle beads to outline each star.

Quilting and Finishing

1. Layer the embellished 2-layered quilt sandwich (right side up) over the backing fabric (wrong side up) on a clean, flat surface. Tape the corners to secure. Use thread or pins to baste all 3 layers in a 3" grid. Remove the tape.

2. Refer to the diagram at left. Use a removable marking tool to transfer the wavy quilting pattern on page 58 to the quilt top. Make 6 horizontal waves.

3. Hand or machine quilt as desired.

⊘⊘

One of the quilting lines shown in the sample runs across the largest beaded star. If you are planning to machine quilt, do not stitch over the bugle bead wall. Instead, stop and restart your stitching as necessary.

In general, it's best not to mark machine-quilting lines too close to beaded embellishments.

⊘⊘

4. Trim the backing and batting even with the edges of the quilt top. Use the 2¼"-wide binding strips to bind the quilt as described in "Binding" on page 40.

ADDING THE DANGLES

1. Place 1 ceramic button at the top right corner of the quilt, making sure that the button's holes are positioned just below the quilt binding. Anchor the button with 6 beaded dangles, using the washer/nut dangle technique described and illustrated on page 25. Use any combination of blue seed and bugle beads to create the dangles, finishing with a blue glass star as the last embellishment on each string. Add additional dangles as desired. Hide the thread knots and stitches behind the button, or under the binding.

2. Add more dangles through the buttonholes, incorporating some of the dangle loops described and illustrated on pages 25–26. Use the white seed beads for these embellishments.

3. Using the remaining ceramic button, repeat steps 1 and 2 to create a second "matching" embellishment in the upper left corner of the quilt.

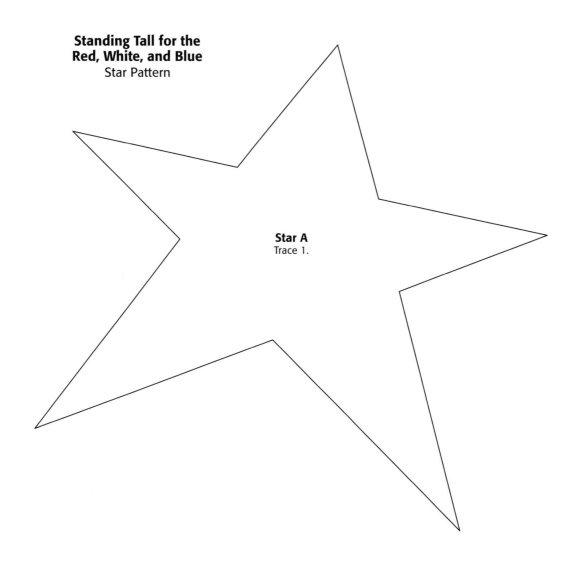

**Standing Tall for the
Red, White, and Blue**
Star Pattern

Star A
Trace 1.

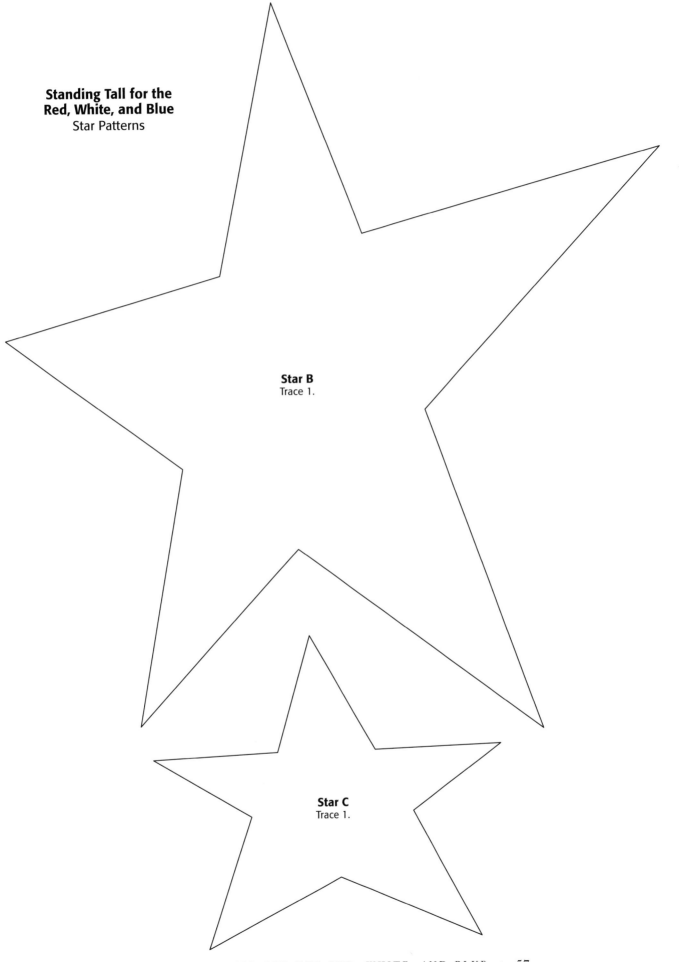

**Standing Tall for the
Red, White, and Blue**
Star Patterns

Star B
Trace 1.

Star C
Trace 1.

**Standing Tall for the
Red, White, and Blue**
Quilting Pattern

Connect at dashed line to complete pattern.

Start

End

Start

BEST FRIENDS *by Mary Stori, 2000, Brodhead, Wisconsin, 21¼" x 17½".*
The hearts are embellished with spirals, Xs and Os, and words stitched with matte-finish seed beads.
Black twisted bugle beads outline each heart.

Wouldn't you love to make this charming embellished quilt for your best friend?

It's such a fun way to say you care!

❀❀

Finished Quilt Size: 21 ¼" x 17 ½"

Materials

42"-wide fabric

- ½ yd. green fabric for background, hearts B and C, and binding
- ½ yd. yellow fabric for background, heart A, and binding
- ¼ yd. black-print fabric for sashing
- ⅝ yd. fabric for backing
- 23" x 19" piece of batting
- 2 pieces lightweight, iron-on adhesive, one 6" x 10" and one 8" x 11"
- Black 30-weight embroidery thread
- 200 green matte-finish seed beads, size #11*, for heart A
- 500 yellow matte-finish seed beads, size #11*, for hearts B and C
- 140 black twisted bugle beads, ¼" long, size #3*, for edges
- Nymo beading thread to match or complement embellishments
- Sewing thread to match fabric
- Invisible monofilament thread for machine quilting

* Available from TWE/BEADS. See "Resources" on page 94.

Cutting

All measurements include ¼"-wide seam allowances.

From green fabric, cut:
- 1 rectangle, 10½" x 14½", for background
- 1 rectangle, 6" x 10", for hearts B and C
- 2¼"-wide strips for binding**

From yellow fabric, cut:
- 2 squares, each 6¾" x 6¾", for background
- 1 rectangle, 8" x 11", for heart A
- 2¼"-wide strips for binding**

From black print fabric, cut:
- 2 strips, each 2" x 14½", for sashing
- 2 strips, each 2" x 13½", for sashing
- 3 strips, each 2" x 6¾", for sashing
- 1 strip, 2" x 17½", for sashing

From backing fabric, cut:
- 1 piece, 23" x 19", for backing

** *The total length of the yellow and green binding strips should equal approximately 90".*

ASSEMBLING THE QUILT

1. Following the manufacturer's instructions, fuse the 6" x 10" piece of iron-on adhesive to the wrong side of the 6" x 10" green fabric rectangle. Fuse the 8" x 11" piece of iron-on adhesive to the wrong side of the 8" x 11" yellow fabric rectangle.

2. Use a black permanent pen to trace heart patterns A, B, and C (pages 63–64) onto white paper.

3. With the aid of a light box, use a removable marking tool to transfer the outline and beading design for heart A onto the right side of the yellow fused fabric. Repeat to transfer the outlines and beading designs for hearts B and C onto the right side of the green fabric. Cut out all 3 hearts on the traced lines.

4. Refer to the quilt photo on page 59 and the assembly diagram below for guidance. Center the yellow heart (A) on the 10½" x 14½" green fabric rectangle, fusible side down. Follow the manufacturer's instructions to fuse the heart in place. Repeat to center and fuse a green heart (B and C) on each of the 6¾" yellow fabric squares.

Quilt Assembly Diagram

Some marking tools are affected by the application of a hot iron, making the marks difficult—if not impossible—to remove. Always test your marking tools, and wait until the hearts are fused in place before transferring the beading designs if necessary.

5. Use your sewing machine and black embroidery thread to sew a blanket stitch around the edge of each heart.

Machine blanket stitch

6. Refer to the assembly diagram at left. Sew a 2" x 14½" black sashing strip to opposite long sides of the 10½" x 14½" heart A rectangle. Press seams toward the strips. Sew a 2" x 13½" black sashing strip to the top and bottom edges of the block. Press.

7. Arrange the three 2" x 6¾" black print sashing strips and the 6¾" heart B and heart C squares to make a vertical row as shown in the assembly diagram. Pin and sew the strips and blocks together, and press seams toward the strips.

8. Referring again to the assembly diagram, arrange the units from step 6 and step 7 and the 2" x 17½" black sashing strip as shown. With right sides together, and long raw edges aligned, pin and sew the units and strip together to complete the quilt top. Press seams toward the sashing strips.

EMBELLISHING AND FINISHING

1. Bead the marked designs on each heart using the straight-line beading technique described and illustrated on page 17 and the curved-line beading technique shown on page 18. Use the green matte beads for heart A, and the yellow matte beads for hearts B and C.

2. Layer the backing (wrong side up), batting, and beaded quilt top (right side up) on a clean, flat surface. Tape the corners to secure, and thread baste the three layers in a 3" grid. Remove the tape.

3. Refer to the quilt photo on page 59. Use a removable marking tool and ruler to mark a grid of diagonal quilting lines 1½" apart over the quilt top. Do not mark in the hearts.

4. Machine or hand quilt, following the marked 1½" grid.

5. Randomly piece the 2¼"-wide yellow and green binding strips to make a single 90" (approximately) length of binding. Trim the batting and backing even with the edges of the quilt top, and bind the quilt as described in "Binding" on page 40.

6. Refer to the quilt photo on page 59. Use the basic bead stitch as described and illustrated on page 15 to sew evenly spaced black bugle beads all around the perimeter of each heart, ⅛" from the edge. Space the beads ¼" apart around heart A and ½" apart around hearts B and C. Don't be afraid to make tiny spacing adjustments as you bead, if necessary.

If you are a true type A personality, you may want to mark where the bugle beads should be placed. (I just eyeballed it, even though I'm a certified A!) There's no need to tie off after each bead; just pass the needle through between the quilt top and batting, coming up where the next bead should go. This provides a neater appearance on the back of the quilt because the beading thread is hidden between the layers.

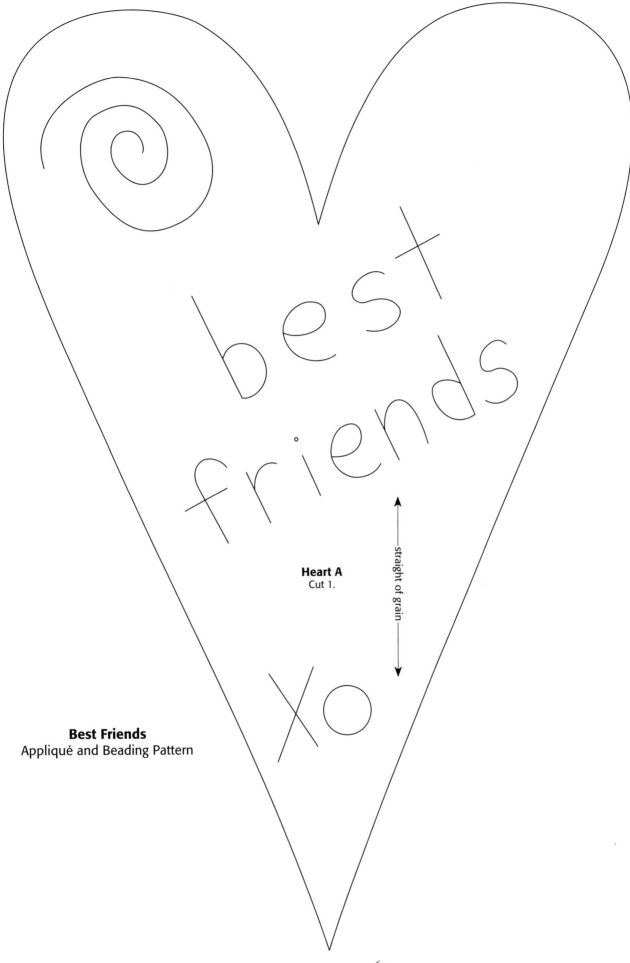

best friends

Heart A
Cut 1.

straight of grain

xo

Best Friends
Appliqué and Beading Pattern

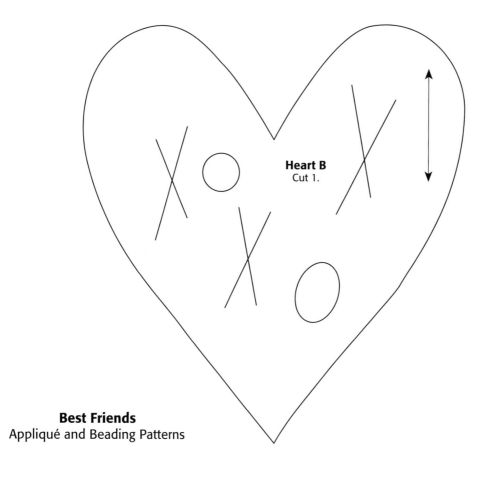

Heart B
Cut 1.

Best Friends
Appliqué and Beading Patterns

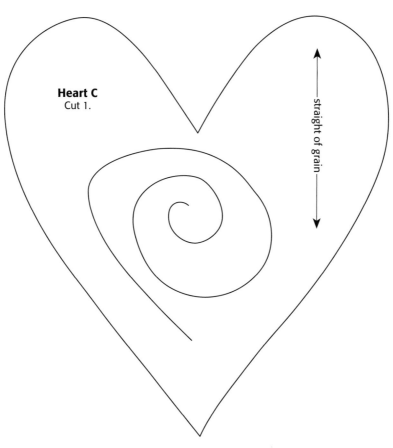

Heart C
Cut 1.

straight of grain

Dairy Christmas

Dairy Christmas by Mary Stori, 1995, Brodhead, Wisconsin, 12½" x 12½".
On this whimsical quilt, sparkly star sequins attached with seed beads represent falling snow.

My work often features Holstein cows and a play on words (or two).
This design became a quilted Christmas "card" for a few dear friends. The fabrics and color choices
are provided as a guide. Feel free to substitute with fabric scraps you have on hand.

᠖᠖

FINISHED QUILT SIZE: 12½" X 12½" (APPROXIMATELY)

MATERIALS

- 13" x 9" strip white-on-white fabric for snow
- 13" x 8" strip blue fabric for sky
- 2 squares, each 5" x 5", green print fabric for tree (H)
- 2" x 2" square brown Ultra Suede or craft felt for horn (A) and tree trunk
- 7" x 7" square black and white spotted fabric for cows (B, C)
- 3" x 3" square pink Ultra Suede or craft felt for noses and udders (D, E, F)
- 2" x 3" square red plaid homespun fabric for hat (G)
- 2 squares, each 5"x 5", muslin for cartoon bubbles (I and J)
- 2 strips, each ½" x 6", colorful homespun fabric for scarves, torn so short edges fray
- 14" x 14" square for backing
- ¼ yd. red plaid fabric for binding
- 14" x 14" square batting
- 8 black seed beads, size #10 or #11, for cow embellishment
- 4 round white sequins for cow eyes
- 1 small brass bell for tip of hat (and seed bead to attach it)
- 50 small white star sequins for snowflakes
- 60 white seed beads, size #10 or #11, for snowflakes
- Twin sewing machine needle, size 2.0

- Assortment of regular sewing and decorative threads
- Open-toe machine embroidery foot (optional)
- 5" x 5" square lightweight iron-on adhesive
- Fine-point permanent pen
- Freezer paper
- Red permanent pen
- 1½"-wide length of narrow black ribbon or cord for cow tail
- Nymo beading thread: white

MAKING THE QUILT TOP

MY ARRANGEMENT FOR this design should be considered only a guideline. Feel free to place the motifs wherever you like. Refer to the quilt photo on page 65 and "Sewing Skills" on page 39 for guidance as needed.

1. Equip your sewing machine with a 2.0 twin needle threaded with 2 spools of decorative thread. (A twin needle creates a tuck in the fabric, adding texture.) Place white sewing or bobbin thread in the bobbin, and for better visibility, install an open-toe embroidery foot if you have one.

2. Press the 13" x 9" white-on-white fabric well. Stitch 4 or 5 curvy lines across the 13" width of the fabric to create the appearance of snow banks.

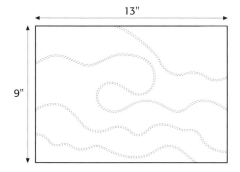

3. Use a removable marking tool to draw a gentle curve across the 13" width on the lower edge of the 13" x 8" blue sky fabric. Trim away the excess below the line, retaining a scant ¼"-wide seam allowance.

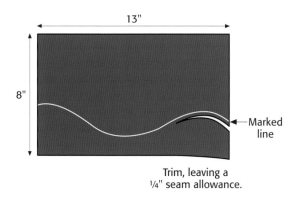

Trim, leaving a
¼" seam allowance.

4. Lay the white-on-white textured snow fabric right side up on a table. Position the sky fabric, right side up, with the cut curved edge

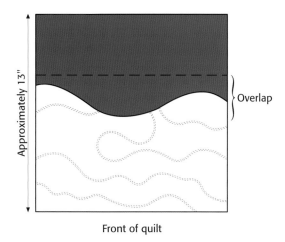

Front of quilt

overlapping the top edge of the white fabric. Make sure there is an adequate amount of "snow" fabric beneath the curve to accommodate the seam allowance on the curved edge of the appliqué. The entire piece should measure about 13" square. Pin or thread baste in place.

5. Use matching blue thread to hand appliqué the bottom curved edge of the sky to the snow fabric, turning the seam allowance under along the marked line. Turn the stitched piece to the wrong side and trim away any excess white fabric behind the sky, retaining a ¼"-wide seam allowance.

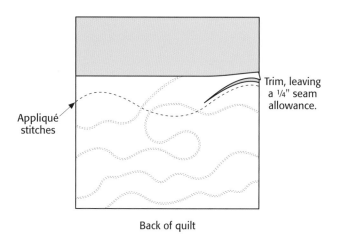

Back of quilt

6. Following the manufacturer's instructions, fuse the iron-on adhesive to the wrong side of one 5" square of green fabric. Fuse the square to the wrong side of the second 5" green square.

7. Refer to the patterns on pages 69–70. Use a fine-point permanent pen to trace 1 each of appliqué patterns A–C and E–J, and 2 of pattern D, onto the dull side of a large piece of freezer paper. Cut out each pattern on the traced line.

8. Place the freezer paper templates for appliqués A, D–F, and H, shiny side down, onto the wrong side of the appropriate fabric as shown in the materials list on page 66. Use a

warm, dry iron, and a pressing cloth if necessary, to press the templates onto the fabric.

9. Use small, sharp scissors to cut out the appliqués on the traced lines. Cut a ¼" x 1½" strip for the tree trunk from the remaining scrap of brown Ultra Suede. Fray the edges of the tree branches if desired.

10. Use a fine-point removable marking tool to trace the remaining freezer paper templates onto the right side of the appropriate fabrics. Cut out the appliqués, adding a scant ¼"-wide seam allowance.

11. Referring to the patterns on pages 69–70, use a fine-point red permanent pen to write the messages on cartoon-bubble appliqués I and J. You may also choose to machine stitch the messages in red thread, as I did.

12. Referring to the placement diagram below and the quilt photo on page 65 for suggestions, arrange the appliqués on the quilt top to your satisfaction. Remember to tuck the horn and udders under the cows. Also wrap and tie the ½" x 6" homespun scarves around the cows' necks, and position the 1½" cord or ribbon tail on cow B. Thread or pin baste the pieces to the background.

13. With the exception of the tree (H), hand appliqué all the pieces in place, including the tree trunk. Machine sew a straight stitch down the lengthwise center of the tree to secure it to the quilt. To secure the hat (G), appliqué the entire bottom edge or fray the edge to leave unfinished. Appliqué the 2 side edges to the halfway point. Twist the top so that the tip points downward and appliqué it in place.

Placement Diagram

EMBELLISHING

1. To stabilize the project for beading, thread baste the batting to the wrong side of the quilt top in a 3" grid. You will now be treating these 2 layers as 1 layer.

2. Use 2 black seed beads and the basic bead stitch described and illustrated on page 15 to add nostrils to each cow's nose. Use 2 black seed beads, 2 white sequins, and the washer/nut method shown on page 21 to give each cow 2 eyes. Use the washer/nut method shown on page 22 to secure the small bell to the end of the hat with the appropriately sized seed bead.

3. Refer to the quilt photo on page 65. Use the star sequins and white seed beads, the scatter stitch zigzag method shown on page 20, and the washer/nut method shown on pages 21 to scatter "snowflakes" randomly over the sky and snow. Add any remaining white beads as desired. The beading holds the batting to the quilt top, much like tying a quilt. Because the project is quite small, there is no need to quilt it.

FINISHING

1. Remove the basting thread. Layer the embellished 2-layer quilt sandwich (right side up) over the backing (wrong side up) on a clean, flat surface. Tape the corners to secure, and thread or pin baste to secure the layers for binding. Remove the tape.

2. Trim the backing and batting even with the edges of the quilt top. Cut two 2¼" x 42" strips from the red plaid fabric. Use the strips to bind the quilt as described in "Binding" on page 40.

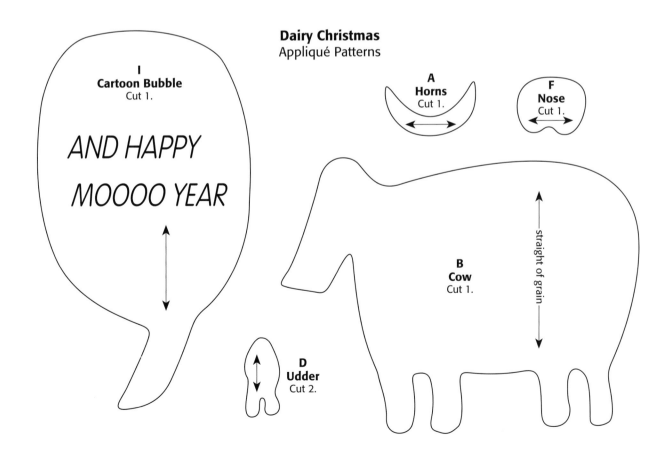

Dairy Christmas
Appliqué Patterns

I
Cartoon Bubble
Cut 1.

AND HAPPY

MOOOO YEAR

A
Horns
Cut 1.

F
Nose
Cut 1.

B
Cow
Cut 1.

straight of grain

D
Udder
Cut 2.

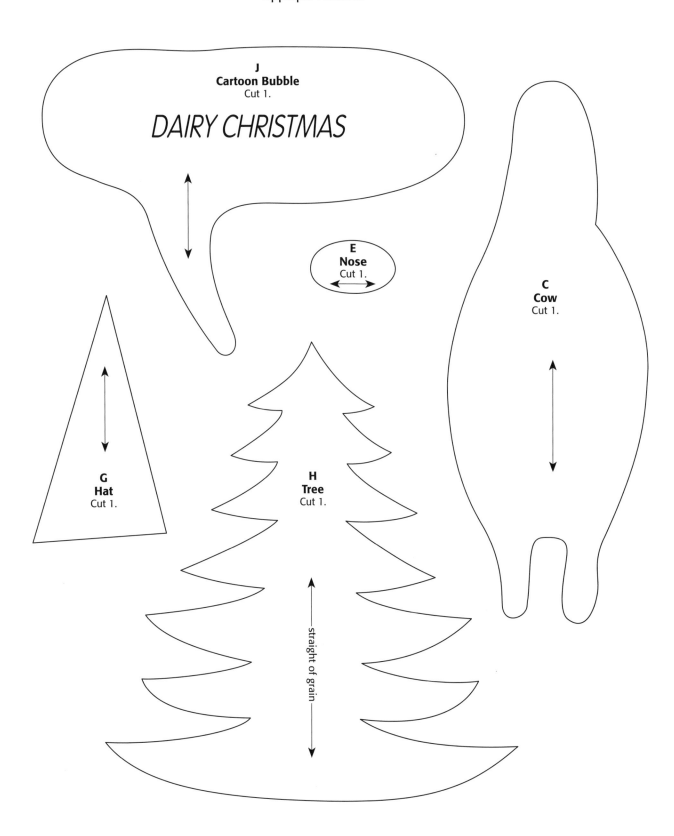

BRAIN CRAMPS *by Mary Stori, 1999, Brodhead, Wisconsin, 30" x 30".*
I beaded old watch faces to the quilt to convey the sense of time passing too quickly.

After enduring endless good-hearted teasing by my husband
about the fretting and agonizing I put myself through during the process of building our house,
this quilt nearly leapt out of my hands! The stress turned into laughter
as I worked on the piece!

❧❧

Finished Quilt Size: 30" x 30"

Materials

42"-wide fabric

- 8 strips, each 14" x 5", of different-colored solid fabrics for arrows
- 11" x 11" square red or pink fabric for face
- 1⅞ yds. black and white fabric for quilt top and backing
- ¼ yd. black Ultra Suede or craft felt for clock hands and lettering
- ⅛ yd. *each* of 8 coordinating print fabrics for nose, triangles, and binding
- 33" x 33" square of batting
- 40 yellow seed beads, size #10 or #11, for tacking rickrack
- 2 large decorative beads for eyes (and 2 seed beads large enough to secure them)
- 2 yds. yellow rickrack for embellishment
- 20–25 watch faces and hands for embellishment (and 20–25 seed beads large enough to secure them)
- Black permanent pen
- Freezer paper
- Alphabet and numerical (0–9) rubber stamp set with ½" figures
- Black permanent textile ink
- Black embroidery floss
- Nymo beading thread: gray or white
- Sewing thread to match fabrics

Cutting

All measurements include ¼"-wide seam allowances.

From black and white fabric, cut:

- 1 square, 30" x 30", for background
- 1 square, 33" x 33", for backing

Assembling the Quilt Top

Refer to "Sewing Skills" on pages 39–41 as needed.

1. Referring to the patterns on pages 76–78, use a black permanent pen to trace 1 each of appliqué patterns A–H (arrows) onto the dull side of a large sheet of freezer paper. Cut out each paper arrow on the traced lines. When you have decided upon the color arrangement for the arrows, use a removable marking tool to trace the appropriate paper template carefully onto the right side of the desired 14" x 5" strip of solid colored fabric. Cut out each fabric arrow, adding a scant ¼"-wide seam allowance. Remove, but retain, the freezer paper.

2. Use a black permanent pen to trace face appliqué pattern I (pages 75–76) onto white paper. With the aid of a light box, use a removable marking tool to transfer the outline and embellishing lines onto the 11"

square of red or pink fabric. Cut out the face, adding a scant ¼"-wide seam allowance.

3. Place the circle of face fabric on a hard surface that has been protected with paper. Following the manufacturer's instructions, use the textile ink and numerical rubber stamps to stamp the clock numbers on the face. Refer to the quilt photo on page 71 and the face-placement diagram below for guidance as needed. You may want to practice on a scrap of fabric first. Use the textile ink and the side and tip of a wooden toothpick to imprint the "minute" lines and dots on the face as shown, and heat set the ink if necessary.

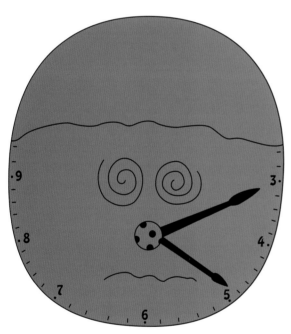

Placement Diagram
Face

4. In a similar fashion, use the alphabet stamps to stamp your "personal worries" onto the 8 fabric arrows. Completing this step now, rather than after the arrows have been appliquéd, provides the opportunity to redo an arrow if needed. (See tip at right.)

@/@

It's a good idea to practice on the freezer-paper arrow templates to get comfortable with the placement and spacing of the lettering before you commit ink to fabric.

@/@

5. Place the rubber-stamped face in an embroidery hoop. Refer to the placement diagram and embroider the hairline, eyes, and mouth using the outline stitch and 3 strands of black embroidery floss.

6. Fold the 30" square of black and white fabric in half vertically and horizontally to find its center point. Mark the center on the wrong side with a straight pin. Likewise, fold the face in half in 2 directions to find its center, and mark with a straight pin. Match the center point of the face with the center point of the quilt top, and thread baste the face in place.

7. Hand appliqué the face to the quilt. If the background fabric shadows through the appliqué, trim it away, retaining a ¼" seam allowance.

8. Tie knots in the rickrack at random intervals. Bead appliqué it to the face above the hairline.

9. Refer to the patterns on pages 76 and 79–80, and trace appliqué pattern J (clock hands) and the lettering for the words *Brain Cramps* onto the dull side of a large piece of freezer paper. Cut out on the traced lines. Use a warm, dry iron and a pressing cloth to press the freezer paper patterns shiny side down onto the wrong side of the black Ultra Suede or felt. Cut out the shapes right along the edge of the paper. Remove and discard the freezer paper.

10. Use a removable marking tool to draw a total of 25–30 small triangular shapes—any size you please—on the 8 coordinating print fabrics. (Don't obsess about this; I made no attempt to make mine perfectly even.) Transfer 1 nose appliqué pattern K (page 76) onto one of the print fabrics. Cut out the nose and the triangles, adding a scant ¼"-wide seam allowance.

11. Referring to the photo on page 71, position all the prepared appliqué designs in their appropriate positions. Randomly scatter the triangles on the quilt top, surrounding the face and arrow appliqués. Using thread to match the appliqué fabric, hand appliqué the pieces.

FINISHING AND EMBELLISHING

1. Layer the backing (wrong side up), batting, and quilt top (right side up) on a clean, flat surface. Tape the corners to secure, and pin or thread baste in a 3" grid. Remove the tape.

2. Machine or hand quilt in a design of your choice. I echo quilted around the arrows and lettering, avoiding the small appliqué triangles wherever possible.

3. Trim the backing and batting even with the edges of the quilt top. Use remaining scraps of the 8 coordinating print fabrics to cut 2¼"-wide binding strips to total approximately 135" in length. Piece the strips and use them to bind the quilt as described in "Binding" on page 40.

@ @

Ordinarily the binding is added last, but to prevent the watch parts from snagging on the quilt (or the quilter), I determined it was better to add it earlier.

@ @

4. Refer to the quilt photo on page 71. Use the washer/nut method described and illustrated on page 21 to secure the eyes, watch faces, and hands to the quilt with appropriately sized seed beads. To keep the beading thread and knots from showing on the back, pass the needle between the quilt top and batting only, hiding the knots under the embellishments.

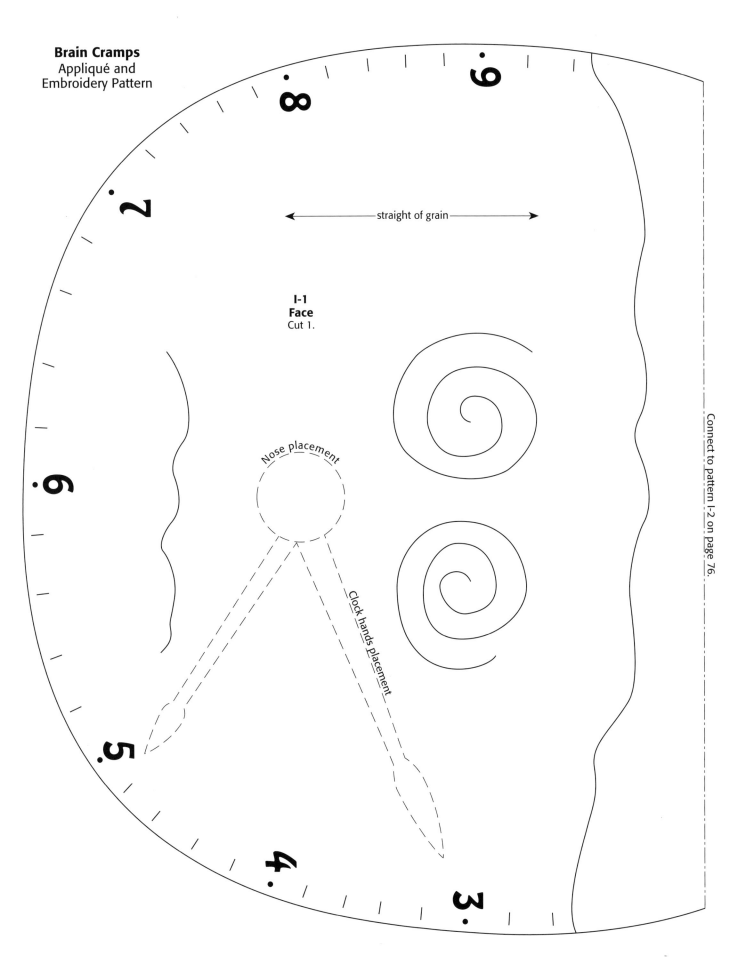

Brain Cramps
Appliqué and
Embroidery Pattern

I-1
Face
Cut 1.

straight of grain

Nose placement

Clock hands placement

9

8

7

6

5

4

3

Connect to pattern I-2 on page 76.

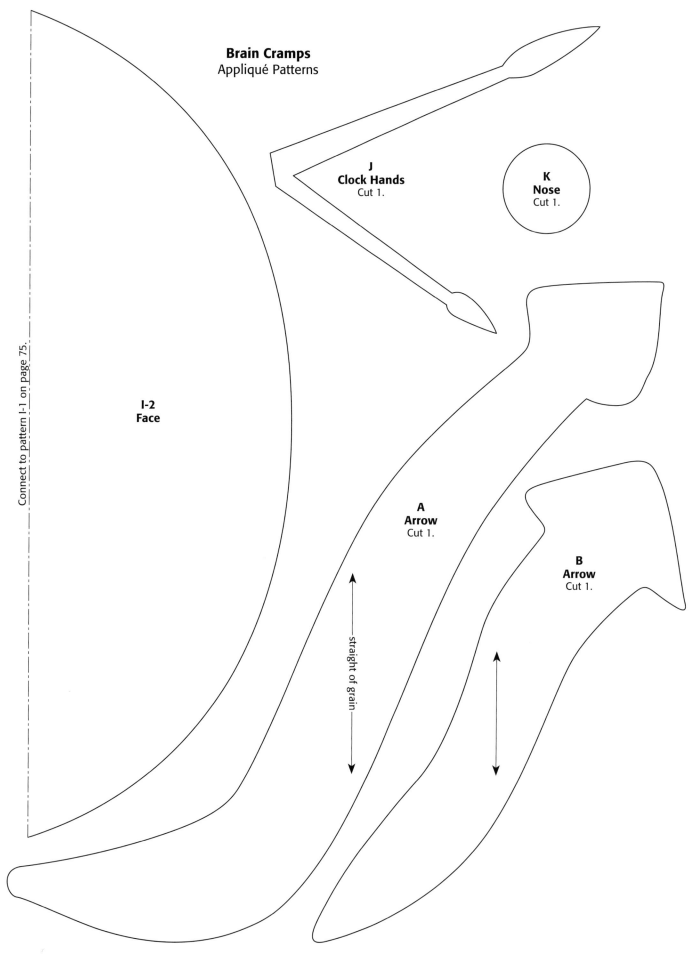

Brain Cramps
Appliqué Patterns

Connect to pattern I-1 on page 75.

J
Clock Hands
Cut 1.

K
Nose
Cut 1.

I-2
Face

A
Arrow
Cut 1.

B
Arrow
Cut 1.

straight of grain

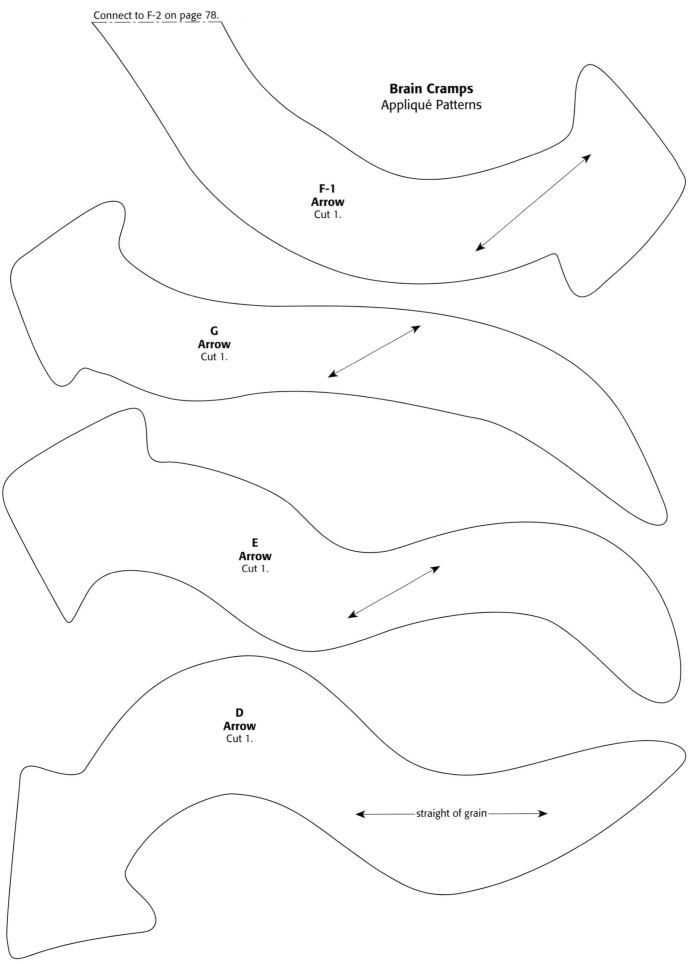

Connect to F-2 on page 78.

Brain Cramps
Appliqué Patterns

**F-1
Arrow**
Cut 1.

**G
Arrow**
Cut 1.

**E
Arrow**
Cut 1.

**D
Arrow**
Cut 1.

straight of grain

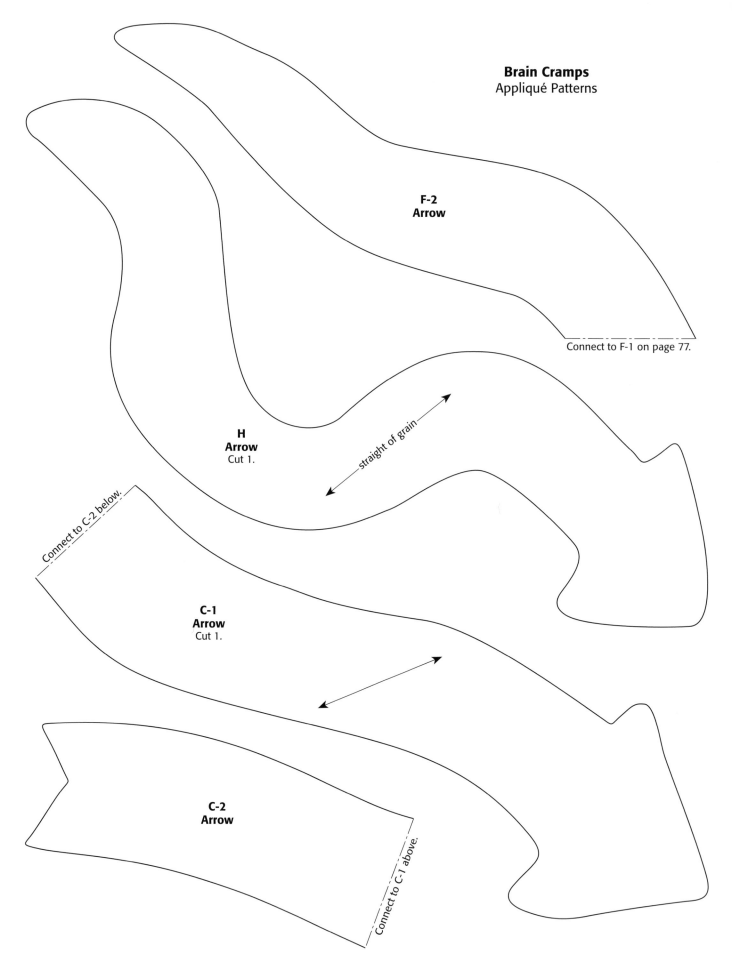

Brain Cramps
Appliqué Patterns

F-2
Arrow

Connect to F-1 on page 77.

H
Arrow
Cut 1.

straight of grain

Connect to C-2 below.

C-1
Arrow
Cut 1.

C-2
Arrow

Connect to C-1 above.

Cut 1.

Cut 2.

Cut 2.

Cut 1.

Brain Cramps
Appliqué Patterns

Cut 1.

Cut 1.

Cut 1.

Brain Cramps
Appliqué Patterns

Cut 1.

Cut 1.

Cut 1.

Cut 1.

Tropical Fish Sticks *by Mary Stori, 1999, Brodhead, Wisconsin, 15½" x 18".*
Embellishments, created with a variety of beading techniques, carry out the theme of this fun wall quilt.

My position as quilt tour host for Specialty Tours has provided abundant inspiration for me. This small wall quilt was a workshop project designed to teach my embellishment techniques on a Caribbean cruise. (Hey, someone has to do it!) In creating the three-dimensional fish you will learn a fun new technique.

❀❀

FINISHED QUILT SIZE: 15½" x 18"

MATERIALS

42"-wide fabric

- 1 yd. turquoise "water" fabric for quilt top, backing, and binding
- 5 fish shapes of various colors and sizes, cut from conversation or theme fabric and including a minimum 1"-wide seam allowance*
- 6" x 6" square of gray fabric for stone base
- 4" x 2" strip of tan Ultra Suede or craft felt for fish skeleton
- ¼" x 42" strip of brown Ultra Suede or craft felt for "sticks"
- 17" x 20" piece of 80/20 cotton-poly batting
- 40 *each* of 4 different-color seed beads, size #10 or #11**, for fish embellishment
- 40 *each* of 2 different-color bugle beads, size #3**, for fish embellishment
- 50 seed beads, size #10, for fishnet +
- 50 twisted bugle beads, size #3, for fishnet +
- Charms, trinkets, seashells, pearls, and miscellaneous beads for embellishments
- 350–400 white or clear seed beads, size #10 or #11, for waves
- Decorative thread for machine quilting
- Sewing thread to match fabrics
- 1 sandwich-size plastic bag of polyester fiber fill stuffing (not quilt batting)
- Nymo beading thread to match embellishments (or gray)
- Black permanent pen
- Light box

- Gray embroidery floss, slightly darker than the gray "stone" fabric
- Freezer paper
- Roxanne Glue-Baste-It (optional)

* The largest fish I used was 2" x 5", the smallest about 2" in diameter.

** These beads will be used to embellish the fish and other objects. Your fabrics and other embellishment items will ultimately determine the colors and beading techniques, so the number required may change.

+ These should be the same color if possible. I suggest topaz, seaweed green, or brown.

CUTTING

ALL MEASUREMENTS INCLUDE ¼"-wide seam allowances.

From turquoise fabric, cut:
- 1 piece, 15½" x 18", for background
- 1 piece, 17" x 20", for backing
- 1 piece the exact size of each fish cutout, including the 1" margin
- 2 strips, each 2¼" x 42", for binding

QUILTING THE BACKGROUND

1. To prepare the quilt for quilting, use pins to baste the batting to the wrong side of the 15½" x 18" turquoise background fabric. You will now be treating these 2 layers as 1 layer. (You will add the backing later.)

2. Refer to the quilt photo on page 81. Thread your sewing machine with decorative thread, and machine quilt random wavy lines over the entire quilt top, stitching through the 2 layers. The lines should run horizontally (rather than vertically) over the quilt to suggest the movement of the water. About 14 or 15 "waves" should do it. This stabilizes the quilt top in preparation for the embellishments.

ADDING APPLIQUÉS AND EMBELLISHMENT

REFER TO "Sewing Skills" on pages 39–41 for guidance as needed.

1. Place each fish cutout right sides together with the matching piece of turquoise fabric, and pin. Set your sewing machine to a very short stitch (18–20 stitches per inch for American machines, or 1.0 on European machines). With the wrong side of the fish

fabric facing you, sew completely around the fish motif, overlapping the starting point by ⅛". (The 1" margin prevents the raw edges from getting caught in the feed dogs.)

@@

You may need to "clean up" the fish design a little by ignoring some of the sharp points or "skinny" spots as you stitch around its outline.

@@

2. Cut out the fish, leaving a scant ¼" seam allowance. Clip curves where necessary, and cut an opening in the turquoise fabric with small, sharp embroidery scissors. Turn the fish right side out and stuff *lightly* with the fiber fill. Don't make them rock-hard! Whip-stitch the opening closed.

3. Embellish the fish with the 4 different colors of seed beads and 2 different colors of bugle beads. You can use a whole variety of techniques, including the regular and zigzag scatter-stitch method described and illustrated on page 20, the chain stitch shown on page 32, the picot stitch shown on page 32, or the bugle-bead wall method shown on page 33. For inspiration, refer to the detail photos of this quilt on pages 34 and 36. Embellishing the fish now allows you to hide all the knots and threads on the back of the fish.

4. Refer to the patterns on page 85 and use a black permanent pen to trace appliqué pattern A (stone base) onto white paper. With the aid of a light box, use a removable marking tool to transfer the design to the right side of the 6" square of gray fabric. Cut out the shape, adding a scant ¼" seam allowance.

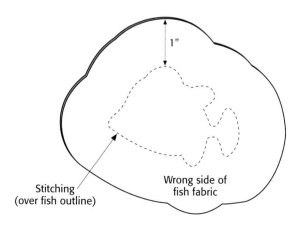

1"

Stitching (over fish outline)

Wrong side of fish fabric

5. Refer to the quilt photo on page 81. Center the stone-base appliqué on the quilted background so that the finished lower edge of the appliqué is about 2" from the bottom edge of the quilt. Hand appliqué in place. Use an outline stitch and gray embroidery floss to embroider the front and side "edge" details of the base, stitching through the quilt top and batting.

6. Use the pattern on page 85 to trace appliqué patterns B and C (fish skeleton) onto the dull side of a small piece of freezer paper. Cut out the patterns on the traced lines. Use a warm, dry iron and a pressing cloth to press the freezer paper patterns shiny side down onto the wrong side of the 4" x 2" strip of tan Ultra Suede or craft felt. Cut out the shapes right along the edge of the paper. Remove and discard the freezer paper.

7. Refer to the quilt photo on page 81. Cut the ¼" x 42" strip of brown Ultra Suede or craft felt into 6 segments of random length (see tip below). Audition possible arrangements of sticks, skeleton, and fish appliqués now to decide the best arrangement. Use Roxanne Glue-Baste-It (see "Resources" on page 94) to hold the sticks and skeleton in place as you hand appliqué them to the quilt. Pin, and then hand appliqué the embellished fabric fish in place catching the back facing only.

❧

Use the size and shape of your fish and skeleton appliqués to determine the length and arrangement of the fabric "sticks."

❧

8. Use the 50 same-color seed and twisted bugle beads, and the bead-net technique described and illustrated on pages 35–36, to bead a fish net on the quilt. You can place the net anywhere on the quilt that you'd like. Refer to the quilt photo on page 81 for guidance as needed.

9. Attach charms, trinkets, shells, pearls, or other tropical theme embellishment items to the lower portion of the quilt. Try a variety of techniques, such as the washer/nut methods described and illustrated on pages 21–22 and the dangles shown on pages 25–26.

10. Scatter beaded waves randomly across the quilt surface. Use the white or clear seed beads and the wave technique described and illustrated on page 33.

FINISHING

1. Layer the embellished, 2-layered quilt sandwich (right side up) over the backing (wrong side up) on a clean, flat surface. Tape the corners to secure, and pin baste. Remove the tape.

2. Trim the backing and batting even with the edges of the quilt top. Use the 2¼" x 42" binding strips to bind the quilt as described in "Binding" on page 40.

❧

You've obviously noticed by now that the quilting doesn't go through to the backing, but that's okay. Because of the quilt's small size, the binding adequately secures the backing to the quilt.

❧

Tropical Fish Sticks
Appliqué and
Embroidery Patterns

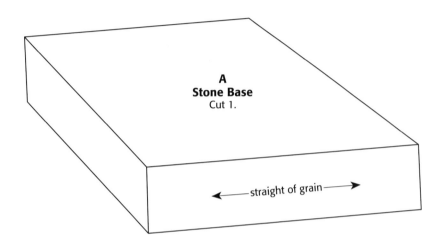

**A
Stone Base**
Cut 1.

←—straight of grain—→

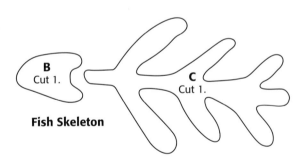

B
Cut 1.

C
Cut 1.

Fish Skeleton

German Goose-Feather Tree *by Mary Stori, 2000, 16½" x 20½".*
I highlighted a simple folk-art design with branched fringe, long bugle bead "candles," and brass ornaments.
The quilt is accented by the red-and-green bead trim that outlines the binding.

This folk-art design was inspired by the primitive tabletop Christmas trees that originated in the German communities of Wisconsin where I grew up. They were made from slender sticks and goose feathers, often dyed green to mimic the look of pine needles.

◎◎

FINISHED QUILT SIZE: 16½" X 20½"

MATERIALS

42"-wide fabric

- ⅞ yd. white-on-white fabric for background, backing, and binding
- ½" x 16" strip brown Ultra Suede or craft felt for tree trunk
- 4 strips, each ¼" x 12", green Ultra Suede or craft felt for branches
- 20" x 24" piece of thin batting, such as Hobb's Thermore
- 190–200 green twisted bugle beads, ¼" long, size #3*, for tree branches
- 14 red bugle beads, 1" long, size #5, for candles
- 15 gold bugle beads, ⅛" long, size #1, for flames
- 15 gold seed beads, size #10 or #11, for tree embellishment
- 10 brass drops, 1" or 1½" long, for tree embellishment
- 4 brass drops, ¾" or 1" long, for tree embellishment
- 1 large gold star charm with hole at top for tree top, and seed bead large enough to secure it
- 6 grams (approximately 1,000) white color-lined seed beads, size #10 or #11, for icicles
- 3 grams (approximately 390) red seed beads, size #10, for binding embellishment
- 6 grams (approximately 900) green three-cut beads, size #9, for binding embellishment

- Roxanne Glue-Baste-It (optional)
- Sewing thread to match fabric
- Nymo beading thread to match or complement embellishments
- Metallic quilting thread (optional)

* Available from TWE/BEADS. See "Resources" on page 94.

CUTTING

ALL MEASUREMENTS INCLUDE ¼"-wide seam allowance.

From white-on-white fabric, cut
- 1 piece, 18" x 22", for background
- 1 piece, 20" x 24", for backing
- 2 strips, each 2¼" x 42", for binding

ASSEMBLY

REFER TO "Sewing Skills" on pages 39–41 as needed.

1. Fold and gently crease the 18" x 22" white-on-white background piece vertically and horizontally to mark its midpoints. Referring to the placement diagram at right, center the ½" x 16" brown Ultra Suede tree trunk over the vertical center, positioning the bottom of the trunk about 2½" from the bottom edge of the background fabric. Secure with straight pins or dabs of Roxanne Glue-Baste-It (see "Resources" on page 94). Hand appliqué in place with matching thread.

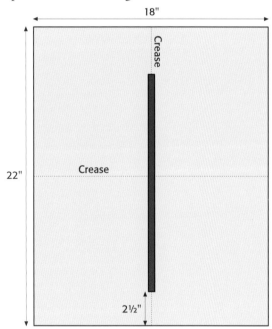

2. Cut the ¼"x 12" green Ultra Suede strips to make one ¼"-wide strip in each of the following lengths: 11", 8½", 6½", 4½", 3½", and 3".

3. Refer to the placement diagram at right. Center the ¼" x 11" strip about 3" from the bottom of the trunk, to form the lowest branch. Secure with pins or glue baste in place. Repeat to position the remaining branches, working from the bottom of the tree to the top with progressively shorter branches. Space the branches about 2" apart.

4. Hand appliqué the branches in place with matching thread. Press well with a warm, dry iron before continuing, using a press cloth to protect the Ultra Suede.

5. To stabilize the project for the beading process, pin baste the batting to the wrong side of the quilt top in a 3" grid. You will now be treating the 2 layers as 1 layer.

EMBELLISHING

1. Bead the tree branches with the green twisted bugles beads. Use the scatter-stitch method described and illustrated on page 20. Be sure to begin with a lock stitch. Use an equal number of beads on each side of the tree trunk as well as on the top and bottom of each branch. Space the beads about ¼" apart, positioning them at a 60° angle to the branch as shown. The placement diagram below indicates the *total* number of beads (top and bottom, both sides of the trunk) on each branch.

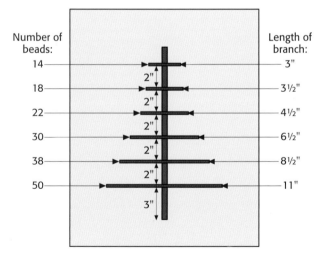

Placement Diagram

2. Bead the "candles" on each branch with the red and gold bugle beads and the basic beading stitch described and illustrated on page 15. Begin with a lock stitch and use a red bugle bead (candle) and then a gold bugle bead (flame) for each candle. Since the candles are spaced rather far apart, it's best to finish each candle unit with a tie-off knot on the back and start fresh with the next one. Refer to the quilt photo on page 86 for placement suggestions.

3. Use the gold seed beads and washer/nut method described and illustrated on page 22 to secure the different-sized brass drops to the lower edges of each branch. Place the drops randomly, arranging them as you please. Refer to the quilt photo for placement ideas. In a similar fashion, use a gold seed bead to secure the gold star charm to the treetop.

4. Use the white color-lined seed beads and the method described and illustrated on page 38 to create branched fringe. "Hang" fringe randomly from the lower edges of the branches to represent icicles. Refer to the quilt photo for placement ideas.

QUILTING AND FINISHING

1. Remove the safety pins, and layer the embellished 2-layered quilt sandwich (right side up) over the backing fabric (wrong side up) on a clean, flat surface. Tape the corners to secure, and pin baste. Remove the tape.

2. Refer to the quilt photo on page 86. Fill in the background with simple wavy lines of quilting. Quilt either by hand or machine, using white or—if you prefer—metallic decorative thread. Stitch from the center of the tree out; in other words, do not sew over the branches or any embellishments. The sample is quilted with 2 lines just above the top and below the bottom branches, with 1 line of stitching between the remaining branches. This is adequate to hold the layers together and provide texture and interest without competing with the main design.

3. Remeasure the quilt, and use a rotary cutter and long acrylic ruler to trim the quilt sandwich to 16½" x 20½".

4. Use the 2¼" x 42" binding strips to bind the quilt as described in "Binding" on page 40.

5. For the finishing touch, use the red seed beads, green three-cut beads, and the method described and illustrated on page 35 to create beaded trim along the seam line of the binding. Refer to the quilt photo on page 86 for guidance as needed.

SUNSHINE IN MY GARDEN *by Mary Stori, 2000, Brodhead, Wisconsin, 38½" x 50½".*
The simplicity of traditional patchwork is combined with the elegance of bead-appliquéd silk flowers
and twisted ribbons for a fresh, new approach to embellishing.

This cheerful quilt features the unusual combination of traditional patchwork and bead appliqué, providing a fresh, new approach to quiltmaking. The silk ribbons, flowers, and leaves add a touch of elegance, and they are easy to work with because of their already-finished edges. My bead-appliqué method makes the process go quickly.

☙☙

FINISHED QUILT SIZE: 38½" x 50½"

MATERIALS

42"-wide fabric

- 1 yd. light yellow fabric for background and border
- 1⅜ yds. medium yellow fabric for background, border, corner squares, and binding
- 1½ yds. fabric for backing
- 40" x 52" piece of thin batting, such as Hobb's Heirloom (80/20, cotton-poly) or Hobb's Thermore
- 6 yds. *each* of 3 different shades of 4-mm wide green silk ribbon for vines and tendrils
- 30–35 purple silk flowers, in varying shades and sizes if possible, for embellishment
- 30–35 green silk leaves, in varying shades and sizes if possible, for embellishment
- A variety of seed beads in assorted colors, size #11, for embellishment*
- 25–30 large seed beads, size #5, for securing flowers and leaves**
- A variety of bugle beads in assorted colors, size #3, for securing flowers and leaves**
- Sewing thread to match fabric
- Nymo beading thread: to match beads, or gray

* The quilt shown includes clear to represent dew drops and colors to match or complement flowers and ribbon. I suggest Mill Hill beads in colors such as Ice Lilac, Dusty Rose, Violet, Buttercup, Royal Plum, Juniper Green, and Christmas Green (see "Resources" on page 94). The number of beads will be determined by beading techniques selected.

** I suggest Mill Hill Pebble beads in colors such as Midnight Rainbow and Pale Pink (see "Resources" on page 94).

CUTTING

ALL MEASUREMENTS INCLUDE ¼"-WIDE SEAM allowances.

From light yellow fabric, cut:
- 17 squares, each 6½" x 6½", for background
- 38 strips, each 2½" x 4½", for border

From medium yellow fabric, cut:
- 18 squares, each 6½" x 6½", for background
- 34 strips, each 2½" x 4½", for border
- 4 squares, each 4½" x 4½", for corner squares
- 5 strips, each 2¼" x 42", for binding

ASSEMBLY

1. Refer to the assembly diagram below and the quilt photo on page 90. Arrange alternating 6½" light yellow and medium yellow squares in 7 horizontal rows of 5 blocks each. Odd-numbered rows begin with a medium yellow square, while even-numbered rows begin with a light yellow square.

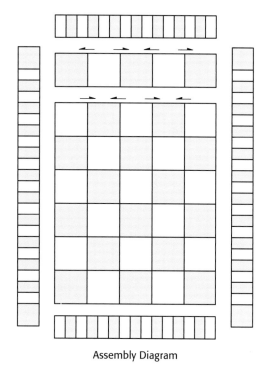

Assembly Diagram

2. With right sides together, pin and sew the squares together into rows. Press the seams toward the medium yellow squares.

3. Carefully pin the rows together, matching the seams; then join the rows and press.

4. Arrange and sew eight 2½" x 4½" light yellow strips, and seven 2½" x 4½" medium yellow strips to make a border unit, alternating the fabrics as shown. Press seams toward the medium yellow strips. Make 2. These top and bottom border units should measure 4½" x 30½". See illustration below.

5. Arrange eleven 2½" x 4½" light yellow strips and ten 2½" x 4½" medium yellow strips to make a border unit, alternating the fabrics as shown. Place a 4½" medium yellow square at each end of the unit. Sew the blocks and strips together, and press seams toward the medium yellow strips and squares. Make 2. These side border units should measure 4½" x 50½". See illustration below.

6. With right sides together, and carefully matching centers and ends, pin and sew a border unit from step 4 to the top and bottom edges of the quilt top. Press seams toward the border units. Repeat to pin and sew a border unit from step 5 to the long sides of the quilt; press.

LAYERING AND QUILTING

1. Layer the backing (wrong side up), batting, and quilt top (right side up) on a clean, flat surface. Tape the corners to secure, and pin or thread baste the layers in a 4" grid. Remove the tape.

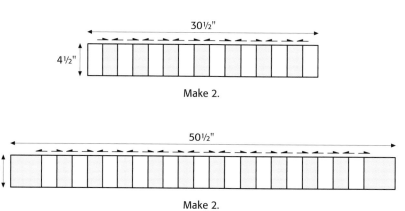

30½"

4½"

Make 2.

50½"

4½"

Make 2.

2. Machine quilt in the ditch, following all of the horizontal and vertical seam lines between the background squares. Continue the lines of stitching into the seam lines between strips in the pieced borders, all the way to the quilt edges. I chose this quilting approach, rather than an all-over quilting pattern, because it adequately stabilizes the quilt, yet provides enough fabric play to allow the bead appliqué to be worked through just the quilt top and batting. If you aren't fussy about threads and knots showing on the back, the beading can be done through all 3 layers.

EMBELLISHING AND FINISHING

NOTE: *Rather than beading this project in a hoop, I found it easier to work with the quilt lying flat on a large table. Check often as you work to be sure the bead appliqué is not distorting the fabric. Adjust when necessary, even if it means redoing a section.*

Most silk flowers have plastic stamens, and leaves may have plastic "veins." Remove these for a softer, more realistic finished appearance—and to avoid having to stitch through plastic!

In addition, the quilt will have a tidier appearance if you take the trouble to hide the knots and threads underneath the embellishments you attach.

1. Refer to the quilt photo on page 90. Use the different shades of green silk ribbon and the various colored seed beads to bead appliqué the surface of the quilt using the technique described and illustrated on page 30. Arrange the ribbons to resemble vines and tendrils meandering around the main body of the quilt and spilling over into the borders. To achieve more interest and visual impact in the vines, try twisting 2 different shades of ribbon together, working with lengths of about 40".

Stick with just 1 strand of ribbon for tendrils, though. Don't worry about hiding the cut ends of the ribbon where you start and stop. These cut ends will be covered later with a leaf or flower, which will also protect the ribbon from fraying!

2. Now the fun part! Arrange the silk flowers and leaves on the quilt in a pleasing manner, being sure to cover the raw edges of all silk ribbon vines and tendrils. Mix any combination of seed and bugle beads you please to secure the flowers in place. Use any variety of methods, including the bead dangle techniques described and illustrated on pages 25–26, the spike technique shown on page 34, and the branched technique shown on page 38. For additional inspiration, refer to the photograph of the commemorative cruise pin (page 27) and the photographs of the details of "Sunshine in My Garden" (pages 27, 30, and 38). Feel free to experiment and create your own flower stamens!

3. Use the colored seed and bugle beads and the scatter-stitch method described on page 20 to attach the leaves to the quilt. Use white or clear seed beads and the scatter stitch to give the impression of sparkling dew, scattering the dewdrops on the leaves as you please.

4. Use the 2¼" x 42" binding strips to bind the quilt as described in "Binding" on page 40.

RESOURCES

Needles and Scissors
Jean S. Lyle
　　PO Box 289
　　Quincy, IL 62306
　　Telephone: (217) 222-8910

Beads
TWE/BEADS
　　PO Box 55
　　Hamburg, NJ 07419-0055
　　Telephone: (973) 209-1517
　　Fax: (973) 209-4471
　　E-mail: info@twebeads.com
　　Web site: www.twebeads.com

Fire Mountain Gems
　　28195 Redwood Highway
　　Cave Junction, OR 97523-9304
　　Telephone: (800) 423-2319
　　Fax: (800) 292-3473
　　E-mail: questions@firemtn.com
　　Web site: www.firemountaingems.com

Mill Hill Beads
　　Gay Bowles Sales
　　3930 Enterprise Drive
　　PO Box 1060
　　Janesville, WI 53547
　　Telephone: (608) 754-9466
　　Fax: (608) 754-0665
　　E-mail: millhill@inwave.com
　　Web site: www.millhill.com

Turtle Island Beads
　　105 Vine Street
　　Baraboo, WI 53913
　　Telephone: (608) 356-8823
　　Fax: (608) 356-5800
　　E-mail: turtle@baraboo.net
　　Catalog available for $3.00

Threads
Web of Thread
　　1410 Broadway
　　Paducah, KY 42001
　　Telephone: (270) 575-9700
　　Orders only: (800) 955-8185
　　Web site: www.webofthread.com

Hand Dyed Fabric
Primrose Gradations
　　PO Box 6
　　Two Harbors, MN 55616
　　Telephone: (888) 393-2787
　　Web site: www.dyearts.com

Sewing Machines
Pfaff American Sales
　　610 Winters Avenue
　　PO Box 566
　　Paramus, NJ 07652-0566
　　Telephone: (201) 262-7211

Roxanne Glue-Baste-It and Appliqué Needles
(Sharps #11 or #12)
Roxanne Products
　　742 Granite Avenue
　　Lathrop, CA 95330
　　Telephone: (800) 993-4445
　　Fax: (209) 983-8798
　　Web site: www.thatperfectstitch.com

Rubber Stamps
Pelle's See-Thru Stamps available from:
　　Purrfection Artistic Wearables
　　19618 Canyon Drive
　　Granite Falls, WA 98252
　　Telephone: (800) 691-4293
　　Fax: (360) 691-5574
　　Website: www.purrfection.com/pelles/
　　　　alphabits.htm

ABOUT THE AUTHOR

Photo by Schroeder Photography

MARY BEGAN TEACHING herself to quilt as therapy while recovering from back surgery in the mid-1980s. She'd planned to return to her career as the owner of a cooking school, cooking instructor, and cookbook author, but after discovering the world of quilting and wearable art, she redirected her energies.

Mary is a lecturer, teacher, author, fashion judge, and quilter whose work has appeared and won awards at national and international shows. She's appeared on HGTV's "Simply Quilts" and "Sew Perfect" several times. Her one-of-a-kind garments have traveled with the 1992, 1994, 1997, and 1998 Fairfield Fashion Shows.

Mary's writing credits are extensive. She's written articles or been featured in nineteen different quilt magazines and publications! In addition to *The Stori of Beaded Embellishment*, her other books—*The Wholecloth Garment Stori* (American Quilter's Society, 1998) and *The Stori Book of Embellishing* (American Quilter's Society, 1994)—guarantee inspiration.

Her work is often humorous, and frequently features fun embellishments and fine hand quilting. She designed the Mary Stori Collection for Kona Bay Fabrics and her own line of trapunto quilting stencils for Quilting Creations. Traveling worldwide as a quilt tour host for Specialty Tours and as a presenter of lectures, workshops, and fashion shows keeps her motivated.

For workshop and lecture information, contact:

Mary Stori
W 811 Taylor Trail
Brodhead, WI 53520
E-mail: dstori@earthlink.net
Web site: quilt.com/MaryS

NEW AND BESTSELLING TITLES FROM

America's Best-Loved Craft & Hobby Books™

That Patchwork Place®

America's Best-Loved Quilt Books®

QUILTING

from That Patchwork Place®, an imprint of Martingale & Company™

Appliqué
Artful Appliqué
Colonial Appliqué
Red and Green: An Appliqué Tradition
Rose Sampler Supreme
Your Family Heritage: Projects in Appliqué

Baby Quilts
Appliqué for Baby
The Quilted Nursery
Quilts for Baby: Easy as ABC
More Quilts for Baby: Easy as ABC
Even More Quilts for Baby: Easy as ABC

Holiday Quilts
Easy and Fun Christmas Quilts
Favorite Christmas Quilts from That Patchwork Place
Paper Piece a Merry Christmas
A Snowman's Family Album Quilt
Welcome to the North Pole

Learning to Quilt
Basic Quiltmaking Techniques for:
  Borders and Bindings
  Curved Piecing
  Divided Circles
  Eight-Pointed Stars
  Hand Appliqué
  Machine Appliqué
  Strip Piecing
The Joy of Quilting
The Quilter's Handbook
Your First Quilt Book (or it should be!)

Paper Piecing
50 Fabulous Paper-Pieced Stars
A Quilter's Ark
Easy Machine Paper Piecing
Needles and Notions
Paper-Pieced Curves
Show Me How to Paper Piece

Rotary Cutting
101 Fabulous Rotary-Cut Quilts
365 Quilt Blocks a Year Perpetual Calendar
Fat Quarter Quilts
Lap Quilting Lives!
Quick Watercolor Quilts
Quilts from Aunt Amy
Spectacular Scraps
Time-Crunch Quilts

Small & Miniature Quilts
Bunnies By The Bay Meets Little Quilts
Celebrate! with Little Quilts
Easy Paper-Pieced Miniatures
Little Quilts All Through the House

CRAFTS
From Martingale & Company

300 Papermaking Recipes
The Art of Handmade Paper and Collage
The Art of Stenciling
Creepy Crafty Halloween
Gorgeous Paper Gifts
Grow Your Own Paper
Stamp with Style
Wedding Ribbonry

KNITTING
From Martingale & Company

Comforts of Home
Fair Isle Sweaters Simplified
Knit It Your Way
Simply Beautiful Sweaters
Two Sticks and a String
The Ultimate Knitter's Guide
Welcome Home: Kaffe Fassett

COLLECTOR'S COMPASS™
From Martingale & Company

20th Century Glass
'50s Decor
Barbie® Doll
Jewelry

Coming to *Collector's Compass* Spring 2001:

20th Century Dinnerware
American Coins
Movie Star Collectibles
'60s Decor

10/00